To fellow
May your path be
with poems and
stars

Lonny Kaneko

COMING HOME FROM CAMP
and
OTHER POEMS

Block 41, Minidoka 1942-1943

COMING HOME FROM CAMP
and
OTHER POEMS

by

Lonny Kaneko

Lonny Kaneko 金子

ENDICOTT and HUGH BOOKS

Endicott and Hugh Books
P.O. Box 13305
Burton, WA 98013
www.endicottandhughbooks.com

Printed in the United States of America

Text and cover design by Masha Shubin
Cover Photo: Sunset © Bluefish339. DreamsTime.com
Author Photo by David Yamamoto

Some of these poems appeared in a fine press limited edition chapbook, *Coming Home from Camp*, published by Brooding Heron Press, Waldron Island, WA, Copyright © Lonny Kaneko, 1986.

Some poems in *You Make My Silence Sing* were included in Camille Patha's Valentine show at the Foster White Gallery, Frederick and Nelson, Seattle, WA, and privately printed, Copyright © Lonny Kaneko, 1989.

Photo from Minidoka Interlude

ISBN 978-0-9894291-5-3

Kaneko, Lonny, 1939-
  Coming home from camp, and other poems / by Lonny Kaneko.

    pages : illustration ; cm

    Some of the poems were originally published in: Coming home from camp. Waldron Island, WA : Brooding Heron Press, 1986.
  ISBN: 978-0-9894291-5-3

    1. Japanese American families--Idaho--Minidoka--Poetry. 2. Japanese Americans--Evacuation and relocation, 1942-1945--Poetry. 3. World War, 1939-1945--Concentration camps--Idaho--Minidoka--Poetry. I. Title.

PS3561.A464 C652 2015
811/.54   2015931270

ACKNOWLEDGEMENTS

The author thanks National Endowment for the Arts for a fellowship during which some of these poems were written.

Thank you to Highline College for professional leaves, which provided the opportunity for research and travel and the time to write some of these poems.

A special thank you to the publishers who first published some of the poems reprinted here, sometimes with changes and revised titles. Thank you, too, to anthologies that have reprinted poems.

Amerasia Journal. "Family Album," "Requiem for John Kazuo Yamamoto."

American Born and Foreign: Anthology of Asian American Poetry. "Renewal," "Lee Siu Long, Little Dragon Lee."

An Ear to the Ground. "Bailey Gatzert: The First Grade."

Asian America. "Reading Water."

Ayumi: Japanese American Publication Project. "Renewal: Algona, Washington."

Breaking Silence. "The Secret," "Coming Home from Camp."

Bridge. "Song for Guilty Lovers," "Street Peddler," "Issei."

The Clearing. "Nothing as Comfortable."

Contact II. "October on Green Lake."

Counterpoint: Perspectives in Asian America. "Rooms."

Crossing the River. "Earthquake Country."

Dissident Song: A Contemporary Asian American Anthology from *Quarry West.* "High Bank," "House of Dreams."

Ferry Tales from Puget Sound. "Departure."

Greenfield Review. "Violets for Mother," "What Can We Lose in San Francisco?"

Homegrown 2. "The Immigrants."

Journal of American Culture. "Million Dollar Myopia."

The Journal of Ethnic Studies. "Museum."

Niagara. "Never Sleep: A Portrait."
Poets at the Faire. "Woodland Park," "Paper, Rock, Scissors."
Seattle Review. "Wild Light," "Letters from Okayama,"
   "Villanelle for Amy."
Turning Shadows into Light. "Camp Harmony: Puyallup
   Fairgrounds 1978/1942."
The Weird World Rolls On. "Falling Man," "Body of Evidence,"
   "Pre-Speech," "Agoraphobia 1955," "Purple Heart,"
   Rushing through Gravel at 99," "Sadness Is Not a River,"
   "Clothes Make the Man."
Western Edge. "Earthquake Country," "Sukiyaki Mama."
The Written Arts. "Beasts from the Heart."

. . . .

These poems are dedicated to those who have walked the path
with me from Minidoka to Bailey Gatzert, Washington Jr. High,
Garfield High School, Seattle Pacific College, and the Univer-
sity of Washington; who were there through church, scouts,
and basketball; who were my colleagues and students at Sunset
Jr. High School and Highline College; who were my mentors,
teachers, my buddies from aikido and tai chi, and my friends
and families in Seattle, Redmond, Vashon, Honolulu, Oregon,
Michigan, Arizona, California, and Shanghai. Whether named
or not, you have had a role in this work.

CONTENTS

INTRODUCTION

One spring day in 1961, Poet-teacher Theodore Roethke walked into our University of Washington classroom with instructions for us to walk out on campus and think back to our earliest memory, and to write about it in prose with as much detail as we could muster. I tried to capture vague memories of seeing smoke on the western horizon of the high plains of Idaho. I saw it in the afternoon and through the evening hours. It was still there in the morning. I knew there was a war against Japan and thought I was seeing fires from the war. Many decades later, I realized I was not seeing the war itself, nor was the view west; instead, I was facing southeast toward Eden, where a fire had burned for days.

Fifteen years later, numerous younger Sansei and Yonsei told me that they had never heard about the Japanese American concentration camps while growing up. It seems their parents never talked about the experience with them. It was off limits. I came to realize that even though no one talked about camp in my house, my parents and I shared the common experience. The secret was something we did not share with my younger sister, who was born five years after the war ended, until years had passed. Thus, Roethke's assignment brought to my consciousness the experience I had long neglected.

Over the next decade, all the activities that fill the beginning of one's adult life filled mine: education, marriage, and job, and what I wrote about shifted from poems typical of the classroom and those of academic poets to recollections of what had followed me quietly throughout my childhood and adolescence. It was natural for me to walk through the doorway that Roethke's assignment had opened for me. That first assignment never became a poem, but it served as the backdrop for a story called "The Shoyu Kid" (1976). The story's publication in *Amerasia*

Journal connected me to the Asian American writers of the 60's and 70's. I discovered there were others who independently had begun to write about their Asian American experiences. Shawn Wong, Frank Chin, and Lawson Inada were among those first connections; they also uncovered the forgotten Asian Americans of previous decades, an important work that demonstrated that the Asian American writers of the 70s were part of a long thread of writers whose work had not received the attention they deserved. In Seattle, Alan Lau was doing important work making Asian American arts and poetry significant to the community. In addition, the 1976 Asian American Writer's conference in Seattle brought an array of writers together.

The poems followed as I became conscious of how the camp experience had shaped my mother's and father's lives, and ultimately mine and my sister's, and by extension all those of my generation and those preceding, who had felt the shame and embarrassment, the oppression of being treated as undesirables when our families were as patriotic as any other American's. I came to realize a quiet paranoia in my family; I grew up being warned to be careful of what I said, to be aware of what others might hear or see or think of me, and to behave in public, for whatever I did would reflect on the whole race. I also remember long, convoluted but engaging letters sent from Japan by my mother's sister. She was a mystery figure whose letters described life in Japan. How did she get there from camp? My curiosity wanted to know more.

A small part in a 1975 production of Momoko Iko's play *The Gold Watch* led to my collaborating with my friend Amy Sanbo on a play called *Lady Is Dying*. *Lady Is Dying* played in both San Francisco's Asian American Theater, run by Frank Chin, and Seattle's Northwest Asian American Theater, with Bea Kiyohara as its artistic director. Working on plays provided me with a background for writing poems with someone else's voice while still tapping into my own experiences. These monologues are truly fictions with the voice being the avenue through which these experiences are conveyed. A few of these are scattered through this book.

The choices for this collection are works that I hope speak to people with a variety of tastes for style and content. This is not a collection with a solid, cohesive theme or style. Indeed, it might be described as just the opposite.

Living on Vashon has put me in touch with life among the living. My forest (not a real wilderness) of animals and daily choice to be face-to-face with elements of nature by simply stepping out my front door has created a life vastly different from the one I had. Living in either the heart of the city or one of its suburbs, I found population, space, and commuting to be the everyday forces that both confined and shaped my life.

I have many people to thank. In addition to those I have already mentioned, I include my parents Lois and Sanny (Sane-tomo) for enduring; my daughter Shayna and her geologist husband Greg and their boys William and Thomas; my son Todd, whose own book of poems was published last year, and his wife, the gifted fiction writer Caitlin Horrocks; my sister Jo Ann and her sons; and my other family of John and Amy in San Diego and their children. Additional thanks to Amy, who suggested I take a poetry course when I needed an advanced writing course to complete my English degree.

Amy's suggestion led me to Theodore Roethke, my first formal poetry teacher, who asked for a sample poem or two the first day of class. I rushed home to write something for class. Even though it was cliché ridden, he let me stay. From Roethke I learned about craft, built a desire to master technical skills and found the courage to face one's demons. David Wagoner and Nelson Bentley were advisors for my poetry thesis, and like hundreds of others, I continued to attend Nelson's evening class for several years. Thank you to all both present and deceased.

I have to thank my friend and colleague Sharon Hashimoto for the correspondences of the 21st century. During our school breaks and sometimes during the summer while I taught, we would exchange poems daily for a period of a month or more. With email available and a midnight deadline, poetry lurked just under the consciousness of daily events, to take on words and form by the end of each day. We wrote haikus, terza rimas, villanelles, sonnets and open, organic forms. Many of the poems in this book were inspired by my reading her poems and challenged by these workaholic marathons. Whether they will stand the test of a single reading or more will be up to you the reader. These sessions provided the opportunity to explore a wide range of subjects and concerns, of style and experimentation, some of which appear here, while many others remain on some computer hard drive. Thanks, too, to Sharon's writing group, to which I have been occasionally invited, and its members: Ann Spiers, Susan Landgraf, John Davis, Bob McNamara, Michael Spence, John Willson, and Arlene Naganawa.

Thank you to artist Camille Patha, with whom I served on the King County Arts Commission. Camille invited me to collaborate on a series of love poems for a Valentine's show she was creating for the Foster White Gallery at the Frederick and Nelson department store. The short poems in *You Make My Silence Sing* are the result of the month or two that we worked together in the fall of 1988.

Sam and Sally Green, my first publishers, have been lifetime friends since their time at Highline College, and published some early poems and the original *Coming Home from Camp*. Brooding Heron Press has a record of publishing great poets and poems. I am honored that they have published mine. I thank them for their support and involvement throughout this process.

Thank you to Ann Spiers, who volunteered to proofread the manuscript, to Apple Cox, who digitally cleaned and enlarged the block photo that includes my family, which is reproduced from *Minidoka Interlude*, the camp memory book, and to David Yamamoto, who provided photos of me.

Of course, thank you to my publisher Jeanie Davies Okimoto, who learned that *Coming Home from Camp* was out of print and decided she wanted to reprint the book. Through her generosity, this larger version is more than five times that of the original. Jeanie has been wonderfully supportive, entertaining, and helpful throughout the process of putting the manuscript together.

PART I

COMING HOME FROM CAMP

ON ORDINARY DAYS

Minidoka Concentration Camp

On these ordinary days that knit
themselves one into another,
there's nothing to do except
close the car doors and cruise
silently down the dust-
bound roads, past clumps
of families sitting on their porch
steps, like regular knots
on a line of hemp. They gaze
at the pall of dust rising
over all the world.

There's nothing to see through
the ordinary eyes that blank out
memories of homes beyond
the fence. They watch the slow
eclipse of sheep across the hills
and enter their single rooms
when the passage is complete.
Though the sheep have left, the people
scuff the dirt in their barbed corral.
The car drives into the horizon
and disappears through the gates
into another morning that
rises just as this one did.

Families secure their losses
in their single rooms. They rope
the quiet progress of their lives
against the ache that gnaws deep.
On occasion someone drinks too much
and the noise floats like lonely smoke
across the evening sky. Ah, the stars!
The dark car coasts up the closest drive,
stops and weighs the unmusical cry

of an ordinary man who feels his son's
fear half a world away.

He can see his son's friends stooped
over him, their hands outstretched
to staunch the bleeding, so they
can tell him he'll be alive,
even though he's flowing
like a sudden thaw. "Stop it!"
the heart cries. "Catch it
in a cup," he cries as the blood sours
a patch of dirt. They're trapped
in a war that forces them to prove
themselves more than anyone
on either side of the fence.
Moonshine *sake* spills the nightmare
over the cup of his sleep.

Over and over. The nights repeat.
Old men fill their days. Their blades
tick seconds against faces
of wood. They knuckle their thumbs under
to brace against the back slice
that shapes a soft curve against
the grain. Women needle their designs
into cloth, a blue bird on a branch,
plum blossoms in the middle of September
thunderstorms, a tiger crouched
among bamboo in the deserts
of December drifts.

BEASTS FROM THE HEART

1

They're here tonight as they always are,
waiting for us to enter their private dark,
their muzzles gray with the digging
that pervades their lives.
They are content to spend their lives
in afternoons that hold no more than dreams.
When we sleep, they test their voices
against the night's blind disorder.

2

I enter the cave, and the mind's voice
heats the soft fat of my childhood.
My stutter shuts off the world
and insures my isolation.
Nothing exists. The eye
mirrors the self. Where
does the beast begin?
As the central figure in the play
it enters disguised
in a house dress, long black hair
rolled into a bun, a tongue
sharp as a row of needles.

3

In December my mother snarled
when she meant to smile. I curled
bearlike in the cave of their lives.

I have sniffed the dank reaches
of the undergrowth.
I have seen the tunnels of moles and gophers.
The blind wanderings of prescient worms
have led to the central root that fed
the barbed circle of her words.

4

Is it enough that the beast
should roll in it and dust my nose in it—
this abstraction of dirt I wear?
The cold is not cold until I admit it;
heat is never sweltering until the mind perspires;
and pain—the cut does not bleed until I look
for blood; the body is too ready

5

Outside the chain-link
preserve is a world for hunters
who reserve the hours between midnight
and dawn to drift into the lives
that surround them. I feel the brush
of wilderness against my thigh.

Midnight! The people who love
me enter their own nightmares;
the chains are lifted,
and I revert to the invisible hunter.
When I howl the world descends.

BUTCHER

1

How little it was and yellow-soft;
   like sunlight in morning
   it walked the plain of her hand

to the ledge of her fingers,
   unready to fly. How fragile
   lost in the fields

of skin. But she fed it,
   her little one from alabaster,
   broken out—and growing

a gawky yellow teenager.
   Gawky and bony
   it was, that never was

worth eating, but amazingly
   avoided cats and dogs,
   being live enough

which means just enough
   to stay alive pecking
   under sticks and drain holes.

When her father drained its blood
   into the garden she felt
   his knife along her throat.

2

   They watch their cage mates
frantic with the smell of blood, their own.
They're tossed to do the barrel dance, drumming
   a once-in-a-lifetime rhythm.

Bathed, defeathered
they blindly circle, a deathly carousel,
skin white and bare as ours. Hands intrude,
    press their bellies,

    poof the unborn, soft
shells, hand warm and lifeless echo
the living body. Down the line
    one hen turns and then

    and then, and then another.
Ten thousand hens—like the daughter's
pet, the living body—wait behind
    the barrel and the cage.

3

He did it all without
a thought of blood or death, the wrenched
neck, the torn gullet, like clipping nails,
    shaving, or taking off

a shoe; day after day, row after row,
    hung meat passed him by,
    a journey he had forgotten he too
is traveling, a softening zero,

    still alive but hardly part
of this, his daughter's life. Trapped
in his personal darkness, the nervous
    trembling of his heart against

the staves of his chest
    frightens him; it's no barrel
    he can laugh at. No emergency
nurse will answer his call.

His daughter circles
the silent post he makes of himself.
A fine steam clouds his eyes.
    She looks for feathers

that speak of angels and a dawny
    stain, finds instead the bloody stain
that gnaws the moons from his fingers.

BAD KNEES HARRY: JAPANESE GARDENER

Bad knees bobbed him across the lawn
like an old nag who'd rather stay
stabled on a foggy morning. Hurry,
he'd say in a flurry of motion
guaranteed to look like action
worth $2.50 an hour. His bamboo rake
whirred through air; leaves flew
and settled where they had begun.
His broom swish-swooshed across
the sidewalk, and grass threshed
the air and settled at his feet.
Here was perpetual motion without effect.
Power mowers growled and grumbled. "Faster,"
he said, "faster. More motion makes
more money." Eyes spied from behind
blind curtains. They paid
to see him dance across the lawn.
And he danced on his knees and
on his feet, in a half crouch, sheep-
shears slicing the garden edging,
his back bent and twisted against
gravity, as if hauled by errant sheep.
Week after week, Harry made money
out of motion. Grass died and grass grew,
but Harry swept and chopped at every blade
until the whole yard shone yellow
like dry summer air.

Violets for Mother

I hear my mother whose hips have
broadened sadly rocking in the chair
that she has re-glued and tied together
twice these past five years.
She is staring through the living room,
older than her mother, her eyes fixed
on the glass that conveys the light and shade
of days. The days are quiet now, straight lines
of sunlight that arrow to certainty and fear
enough to strap one to a rocking chair
for days on end as when she rocked me for ten
and my sister for some twenty years.
Now she rocks all my brothers, unborn
either through abstinence or luck.
Oh, that we could walk to her side or look into her face
and say that we love her,
a chorus of our voices from Minidoka to Seattle,
without unsettling the jungle
of African violets steaming quietly around her,
and in whose presence love
whispers its pink flowers.

ROOMS

1

The old woman lay on an elevated shelf
and held court between my father
and herself. Her mother-tongued syllabic
nonsense filled that room stuffed already with
packing cases, stiff chairs, and steamer trunks,
and echoes even now between my ears.

I was caught in her maze of incense,
unwashed sheets, and mildewed age, hung
like a pendulum above streets
thirsting with homeless Eskimos.

2

I brace against an August wind.
At night hollow horsemen, their drawn swords
gleaming like black hair flowing in the wind,
their teeth yellow in the light of deep alleys,
ride the crossroads of conception and sixty
and raise an incensed silken air
that settles into my clothes.

3

At 70, my father stands between dignity and dust,
a rice paper collage of canneries and pool halls
in Juneau and Ketchikan,
the laundries of Peking and Yokohama,
the barbed wire of Minidoka,
the boredom of nights spent in lobbies of decrepit hotels.

I saw him wrinkle in fields alive with chrysanthemums.
In his dreams he still hangs on lines of conveyer belts
in rooms steaming with feathers and heads.
He is ragged at the edges, empty as an open hand.

4

Dignity can rise from dust,
but not of its own accord.
The caterpillar cries for its own crooked flight.
The struggle outward weaves
its mottled shadow,
like moth dust left on shattered glass.

The old woman is dead now ten years.
Park grass replaces the sagging duplex.
The wooden school stands empty as a skull.
Urban renewal and concrete slab
retirement homes line our treeless streets.

We steady ourselves
beneath a swinging, syllabic sun.
Our smiles cloak the cubicles
we live our lives in,
rooms in which the rocks
of our contentment
rock.

ISSEI
(b. 1889/ d.1965)

His white veined hand shakes out
to touch the dry paper of his own face.
He feels the heart beat in fingers
that probe his inmost secrets.
The drum is beating and he strikes a cymbal,
he strikes a bell, and chants his mandala.
His eyes stare like a lemur's
into a universe of light as limitless
as the intensive care recovery room.

A yak tails into the wind. An ox cart
creaks slowly from the hill village where
lawyers and parakeets are fluttering
through 1907 streets, over dusty pawn shops
and dance halls, behind drapes he has pulled
across his face for ten years in fear
of cancer, diabetes, lunacy.
Saffron. Calamus. Potala. His mind
is robed to the ankles in silk.

His ghost wails into the air-conditioned
atmosphere. They have sliced into his stomach
and sewed him up. His fears are coming true:
there is a lump in his throat
as large as his stomach. The Himalayas
are jagged scars across the sky.
The birds are silent. There are no walls
in his room, no mountains, no sky.
No turning back.

He is floating through a mist
like a leaf in a well of water.
At twenty thousand feet
a flurry of locusts pressed
against the face of a granite scar
whispers, "Welcome. Welcome."

THE SECRET

In memory of Sanny Kaneko 1905-1980

"I heard him fall. He's lying
on the floor," my mother's voice
repeats the words
that carried across the continent.
"Cold when I touched him."
He's gone.
"The ambulance. . . ."
My father's dead.
It's been a year.
I spit the words.
The secret's out.
The garden's gone seedy.
Even the compost knows.
The star magnolia and wisteria, too.
They miss him like a sharp wind
or a thunder shower.

The secret's out.
I wanted him to die
when he was ready,
so I could take his place.
But it's too late,
the spider webs the corners
of his room. My mother lives
with my father's death. He's still
preserved in his wedding solemnity

on her buffet, or laughing
after forty years, about to catch
the ball my mother's tossed. Every night
she feeds his photograph, too busy
with habit to understand
that feeding a man is not
her only freedom.

The truth is, she won't let him die.
She's stuffed him into a cardboard box
and trapped him there.
My heart staggers as his did,
like a drunk spider on a loose thread
against my ribs.
I ignore it until she decides
I should fill his place
behind the wheel of his car
or at the table behind
Sunday's sports page,
my elbows propped like his.

I feel my heart wheeze,
know that I am dying inside,
but I can't let him die either.
I hold him here in my hands—
this skin, nails, no eyes to cry,
muscles that work these words.

"If the ambulance was there on time. . ."
my mother remembers.
Our words work a web around us.
They house our grief.

Father, this is no good night.
Good bye. Good bye.

Renewal: Algona, Washington

My mother prowled like a grave robber
the gray foundation of the vanished house.
Perhaps she found her youth reflected
in the broken glass: her mother like an old country
peasant weeding from sunrise the rows of radishes;
her father fleeing the fallow fields of WW II
and returning to Hiroshima; herself mothering two
baby brothers until they built the neighboring house
which harbors a year-long basement full of water.

On my palm is a scar,
the last sign of having stumbled over the past
into glass that sliced into a mercurial vein
rising like "poison" clear to my armpit.
Behind us, the ribs of the barn
bowed by rains and dry rot, invite air.
Blackberries blot out the neighboring farms.
"Used to be the best farm in Algona," says
the neighbor leaning across the crumbling street.

Three layers of growth camouflage
the farm, but where the gravel of a new road
scraped the edges of the blackberries,
the land bleeds bare soil
and stains my mother's hands where she has nursed it.

Whatever lies there lies like the fire
that once burned under the plowed fields, unseen,
except for an occasional sigh of smoke.
It gnawed for days at the roots of lettuce and corn.

Across the valley, other fields already ripe
with the weight of warehouses, gear factories
and shopping centers are irrigated by blacktopped
country creeks and concrete interstates.
And when we cross parking lots sparkling with rain,

my mother's aging face emerges from the darkness.
Her grandchildren remember her staring
into the dark earth of the farm as if her face
would rise from the past like an old fire.

Family Album

For Charlotte Davis

1939

Picture my grandmother at sixty the year
I was born standing in an old wooden tub
amazed by the shrunken fruit of her breasts,
the dry blossom ends of her nipples
soaking in steamy water.
A slender thread slips through the dark
of her skull like a snake and the room spins
and water rises past her armpits, sweeping
over her like a wave of sunlight.

1940

My grandfather stands in half-drained peat
puzzling over the jigsaw of her face,
which lies like firewood behind the house.
When three-inch corn and beans wilt from a late frost
he sails back to Japan where earth, he says,
is civilized. He dies ten years later
80 miles northeast of Hiroshima.

1942

The locomotive steams over names like Puyallup,
Boise, Twin Falls, and Burley; it heads
where men throw nails and two-by-fours
into desert air. They fall into long lines.
Soldiers empty the cars of names
like Naganawa, Namba, Hiroshige
and prod faces named George, Linc, or Naomi
into rooms furnished with sawdust and sage.

The sign says *MINIDOKA*.
Nobody knows what it means.

1943

My mother waits in line for the laundry tub
she will wash me in; I wait in line naked
while lightning worms through July.
I wait in the midst of our people who say,
"You'll lose your thumbs if you don't eat your crusts,"
and show me hands without thumbs.
A snake winds its way under the sun,
unconcerned, eternal. And the sun drinks us up
like the earth across the yard, never quenched.

1945

Past the gates on our way out,
I see where the water waits.
It is Minidoka dam,
a place for holding the snake
before it falls
into another country.

1965

A king apple's limbs scratch the sky.
The barn sits like a beached whale;
it will survive the next flood and winter
because it is already dead.

Grandfather's house sags with wrinkles,
is tattered with weather.

My father in this country
wears rubber boots
to keep out the blood and water.
But he has grown old, too.
The chickens he bleeds
string across the Pacific.

They scrape down stainless steel belts
to be feathered and return nude,
bottoms up, their bellies empty.

1973

Yesterday Charlotte asked, "Is there still
a bitterness?" Something wormed its way through my blood.
Snake. Water. Earth. "It is a thirst," I say.

Today, in the library a reference book
says that *Minidoka* means *water*.
Water. Something we choke on.

EARTHQUAKE COUNTRY

This poem began when I was born
and continued the next year when you
were born, and found a country full
of earthquakes shaking down our
almost forty years. Tule Lake, ice,
dust, a range of mountains, barbed wire,
Minidoka kept us apart. In Tule,
neighbors pointed their fingers:
"Inu! Inu!" Knives flashed.
West from Minidoka, a far fire
lit the horizon.

After the war they shipped us back
like boy scouts from camp, assuming the doors
of our houses stood swinging open,
that lettuce and beans still filled the fields,
that customers stood waiting for our stores to open.
That long summer at camp became a long winter
full of a hundred faults. Your father raised
apples, deer, chicken, and weeds for other men
until he died from what the war had shaken loose.
My father cut grass on his knees for fifteen years,
waiting for the world to shake a miracle
twenty years long, full of dying chickens.

When your father died, your mother disappeared.
One boyfriend after another tumbled through
your life and faded like childhood down a well.
"We will be here," you said, "after all this
has gone, like two sparrows in a tree
waiting for dawn." You survive your marriage
the way you survived your father's death.

My marriage began in a newlywed world of basement
apartment dwellers who own their own world
but not the floors above, who are flooded
with dripping faucets, flushing toilets,

pot roasts being damned back to dust
and screaming (one day a platter flew
through their window, grew wings,
and wafted down in pieces).

Once I was trapped in a second story
wood-framed flat halfway to the bath,
stretched taut as a garter
between door and floor, caught
between necessities of flesh and gravity.
Like all rubbery beings, master or mastered,
stretched or broken or snapping together,
I straightened on loose legs
in a bouncing bed-braced adolescent world
of shaky geometry and learned, too late,
the amplitude of shock
can flatten me.

I am alone now, the way you were alone.
Divorce islands me from my children.
Your marriage is a continent between us.
Seattle fog and multiple sclerosis
can split us down the middle
but we survive them all
not knowing where the next quake will be.

In this country there are no chairs
to crawl under, no doorways to brace our lives.
No use heading for a bamboo grove where none exists
or hitting the dirt in the open field
and trying to hold the ground together.
We keep our balance,
feeling for the wave.
We ride it out,
our toes hanging over
the shifting plates of earth.

Camp Harmony: Puyallup Fairgrounds, 1978/1942

On November 25, 1978, Japanese Americans from the Seattle area participated in the first Day of Remembrance, a reenactment of their temporary internment in Camp Harmony (a euphemism for the Puyallup Fairgrounds) before being shipped to permanent camps for the duration of WWII.

Western Washington Fair: September 1979

Late September muggy air—young aging mothers ooze
from polyester shorts along the fairway, arms full
of cotton candy and children. Old men in old undershirts
suck cigars. *There may have been love.*

Last Thanksgiving weekend Camp Harmony unsettled
the notes I'd built inside my head.
The empty roller coaster roared, *"Mark this day for history."*
Voices at the microphone, *"My people have been raped!"*

Behind the stamp of Percherons swells the whimper
of children feverish in the rising mud. Fun house mirrors
reshape my children's crabbed faces, bloated balloons
that sail into my arms giggling and ready for more.

My uncle serenaded the milking machines.
The hutched rabbits lie in quiet cages. Plymouth Rocks
squeal like hogs. *Father shaved in the parking lot
and checked his smile before he crossed the open field.*

Mother closed my ears to what snaked through open rafters.
Who stole the flowered crab apples and cherries?
Who stole the ladder? the house? the whole back yard?
The pigs settle into their pink skins.

In their litter of blue ribbons and sawdust, they barely breathe.
Father verified his name and number at the gate.
Mother returned to perking coffee.
Straw-haired teenagers careen like mice down the fairway

years deep in black hair, green tea, barbed wire,
pee, handfuls of rice, and dog turd. I mark this place
for my children's sake. Born in the mirrors
of split levels, they return prisoners
to the fine music of our houses.
I close the door and squint my smile into the other side of evening,
wondering, Whose face will smile back?
Whose crooked tooth will catch the eye?

My grandmother's face sails from a photograph.
I have rubbed my grandfather's ashes in my hands.
I am what I have left to discover.
I am my father's distortion; my children are mine.

Coming Home From Camp

Her Words to No One, 1946

It seems like the same thing all over again.
But worse. One room. Three of us in one bed,
a hot plate, sink, no refrigerator. The milk
spoils on the window sill. The bathroom's public.
I scour the tub twice. And no job.
Daddy can't find a job. He's tried.
The twenty-five they gave us as we left the gate's
not enough for rent, food, and tools.
I've tried the P.T.A. The teachers try
to be conversational. The other parents smile
and look away.

        The farmers in Idaho
were shocked that we spoke English just like them.
They thought we'd be killers, spies who spoke
strange words and bowed a lot. We fixed
our smiles at them when they asked,
"Why have they sent you here?"
Heck, we had just as much right to be happy.
I tried to make the barrack a home and ignore
the racket the coyotes made at night.
You should have heard them. And the thunder.

In this hotel, I look out the window and see
only a brick wall four feet away.
No sky. I guess camp wasn't so bad. At least
we had a yard, even if the fence was there
to keep us in. The menfolk learned to make
tables and chairs, and toys like Mickey Mouse
and Pluto. I learned to embroider flowers and birds
on a branch.

        Here there's the whine of cars and howls
from trains grinding into the station night
after night. There's no reason to say,
"Things will get better." Daddy's got to try harder.

But he won't. Or can't. I never knew
this side of him. After a while you realize
that nothing changes. You don't say, "Keep trying."
You know that nothing changes. It just repeats.
And then you stop. You don't know when it happens.
But it does.

His Words after Work, 1960

Goddammit, she doesn't want to do anything.
She's locked herself in the house and won't go out.
I tell her, "Let's go visit," but she won't.

"Don't have a thing to wear," she insists. "Buy
a dress," I say. "It's a waste," she says, "to cut
twelve inches off a dress to make it fit.
And children's clothes—never."

                              After twelve hours
of work I feel like company when I get home.
Some nights I walk to the drugstore to chew the fat.
I know, I promised to fix the house. It's better
than the old hotel, but needs cupboards and a furnace.
The oil heater's okay. I cut a hole
in the ceiling to heat upstairs, but it's not enough
when it snows. The kid's had mumps, tonsillitis,
and measles for two months straight. We cross our fingers
and hope.

                    She keeps ten years of *Life* in piles,
ten years of *Look, Better Homes and Gardens,*
Good Housekeeping, and now a stack of *Family Circle.*
All we do is eat and read the paper.

Before the war she'd shake the doors with me
in Chinatown. You call it Security:
when the shops closed, we'd go down and make sure.
Got shot once in the leg while eating *udon.*

Saw a Chinaman wave a gun. We slid
behind a table, and I drew mine, but he shot
and ran. Think that's why they gave me a badge
at Camp. Made me captain, because I carried
a gun and kept my peace.

                              I hope there's work
to get us through the week. I hope for something
steadier than cutting grass in summer rain
and bleeding chickens in the snow. Then I think,
It's just as well. I'd hate to lose it all
again. There's less to lose like this. No choice
in those days. Everywhere I looked they said,
"Sorry, you're too old." I was forty-two
and strong enough to last another twenty.

Hell, the truth is, they wouldn't trust this Jap
to keep a parking lot full of cars. It's enough
to keep this house. What can you do but hope
you'll change so they won't say *no?* That's the magic
word, *Change.* You hope it's better for you. You hope
it's better for your son. That's why you work.
You hope or die.

Son's Words to His Teenage Children, 1982

I go alone into the rain, as you must,
a thousand miles from me, past sagging buildings
where *Ba-chan* insists is home, trying to keep
her dying house alive, now *Ji-chan*'s dead.
When I was young, their voices, incessant and empty,
collapsed across the dinner table.
Fear like a .38 followed us from Minidoka.
Worn out and rusty, they sat there cornered
by their own silence. It's as easy to close out
the world as it is to latch a door. The mind dies

in a silence of its own making, and action is chained
by a lock of fear which strangles like a braid
of one's own waist-length hair. Every decision
becomes an unanswerable stutter.

As a child I dozed among the cantaloupes unaware
of barbed wire and guns. Today the Minidoka response
lives in me, passed from mother and father on to son.
There's an animal chained inside, wordless as a bird.

I want you unchained and memorable.
The best gift is freedom. My eyes measure
the chains of this world. The electric fence contains
the fearful, but the mind outleaps loneliness.
I cannot do more than I believe I can.
Like a lake, my own shore despairs the air's freedom,
but the ocean breaks and recedes, its face
an unalterable tide.

I've quit breathing life into lifeless words
that won't stand up and walk. I throw myself
into stoneware, shape and reshape the mindless goo,
trying to find something familiar there.
I'm worn out, rusty from the uncomfortable rain.

This is my gift: we've come a long way from camp:
sometimes like the broken pieces of a stoneware jar,
we're scattered across the floor and forced to make
ourselves at home, wherever we happen to be.

VOLUNTEER

For Dale Hopper at Jerome County
Historical Society Museum, 2005

They huddled together like cattle
on their way to market. Just off the train
when we come up. Heard they'd be here
yesterday but they came today. Shorter'n
I expected. I went up to one little one
and said, "I'm Don. I'll carry your bag."
And the little lady looked up at me, said,
"I carried it from Seattle, I can carry it
the rest of the way." She spoke English,
surprised me sure enough. "Why they
send you folks out here?" I asked. "Thought
you'd be speaking some foreign lingo
I couldn't understand."

          "Of course we speak
English," she said, a little lemon
in her voice. "I was born here just like you
on a farm under storm clouds just like those
thirty years ago."

          I thought about that.
"Here," I said, "I'll take that bag and you
carry your child. Ain't the whole world
gone crazy against you folks!" Thought
they'd be a danger and scary. Not so.
It's a crime, it was. Still is, when I think
about it. That's why I sit in this here museum,
old enough to be an exhibit myself. There's
the high school annual. 1943. See these photos?
Here's the baseball team we played against.
Didn't matter who won, they played
like their lives depended on it. Look here.
Is this you in the front row between your
parents? I was just a young kid. Nineteen.
Your mother, she still alive?

DROUGHT

Face up in the dust,
he feels the tendrils reach
for his face and crawl
across his cheek, tickle his ear,
then slip down the canal
into the deep itch it creates
in its waxy journey. Another strikes
out for the finger twisted
toward the sun, whose heat
has pressed him into the dust.
This cool twist of green
crucifies him in the Idaho heat.
Innocent yet pronounced guilty,
he is invisible.

A chrysalis of thought
has wormed itself too deep
to be scratched and picked.
Settled in place like an old man
in his mountain cave,
it loses its way. This is a child
sewn into the earth,
with a dream full of melons and tulips
that needs only a rainy season
in a country of drought.

ACROSS THE GREEN HILLSIDE

Across the green hillside floated a field
filled with sheep each spring and fall,
a mystery to a child's imagination.
When the sheep disappeared, smoke
billowed like cumulous clouds,
filling the sky, while beyond the far
western shore the war engaged our
collective imaginations. Family camped
against family, citizen against citizen,
trapped in this country or the other.
Right and wrong are clear as sheep
on a hillside, clear as accepting prison
without committing a crime and volunteering
to lose one's life to prove 40
years of family loyalty.

60 years later, I return to the old
barrack door now banished from
the land, and search for that green
hillside that existed so clearly
those years ago. Gone are the sheep,
gone are the shepherds. Gone is the hillside,
disappeared into a child's memory.
So today the world opens downside
up and whatever was right has become
as hazy as a smoky sky, where the war
has materialized in the mind of those
who struggled with the choices of patriotism
or honor, injury, death or renunciation.

Overhead a helicopter roars
toward the smoke, and somewhere I
imagine men dig fire lanes and pump
water from the closest canals. And then
I wonder if the fields on fire

have been fired by farmers clearing
the land after the September harvest.
I won't speak for the farmer who watches
his land burn.

WILD LIGHT

We stand before the long building
others call "latrine," my father and I,
in the dark, looking where stars
should shine but where storm clouds roll
on themselves as they do in time-lapse
photography. Rain strikes like little nails.
A jagged torch catches a still photograph:
our faces upturned to catch the rain
catch the light. The smell of it erases
the new lumber of our room, the dirt
and plaster, the new urine on new concrete.
In seconds, thunder echoes back. Again
and again, lightning follows lightning.
Each flash rips the Idaho sky as we struggle
through dust or snow or rain to pee.

Like folding chairs, we've been installed
in unfinished rooms. My parents have
carried me through the upheaval of rifles,
baggage tags, catcalls and the daily journeys
of the mind into semiarid flats,
until this electric moment. Midnight,
and the child's mind opens. The yellow balloon
they have carried me in pops like thunder.
My father's hand wilts in mine. I am alone
in the storm's passage, dispossessed of bed
and apple trees. Each toy, each dust wisp,
each tricycle track that charts my universe
is shattered by the sharp squeal
of light, the last bark of thunder.

That's when light, like a wild hare,
darting through sage, in a rattle-
struck leap, lifts itself free
of the damp sack of land. In the eye
of light is a will sky wide and deep
as darkness. My leap, brief as the hole

lightning makes in the sky, is free
of barbed wire and any brimstone cup
of words. I am pursued by the mystery
that rushes nameless across the desert
after its own blinding imagination.

How the World Changed after
Grandfather Returned to Japan in 1939

Grandfather never stayed to chat the day
he waved me naked into the nurse's arms.
He left because the land had swallowed his wife
and spit back children whose Japanese limped
the way English stumbled around his teeth.
His children never saw the sun rising
or setting behind his eyes. Life rooted him
in carrots and unions, trapped him while his thumb
was sliced away, while the law wiped him like sweat
from the bald land. He missed the years
we spent behind barbed wire: three of his children
have housed themselves in this promised land;
his fourth followed him—in anger or love,
I wonder.

Straight from Tule Lake, my seamstress aunt
sailed to Okayama after the bomb
to clothe her father in mutual poverty.
Her letters record in December's death, earth
was shaken by uncertain trembling. Wind
and rain numbed their fingers and words, while those
a *ken* away, crushed by a shuddering glare
of light, suffered a mysterious heat in the bone
that would in turn turn blood against itself.
While neighbors survived by saving hulls of rice
and barley for broth, Grandfather drank soup
of cloth soaked in water, warmed. My aunt believed
the world caretaker would cart her father
through pneumonia, diarrhea, and starvation.

In America, Father borrowed through
another jobless winter, and sent New Year's
Eve an empty package to celebrate their hope.
I sat at breakfast a world from everyone,
and stared at an egg's unblinking eye.
"Eat your breakfast," my mother said as fog

obscured telephone lines that had yet to ring
me across the wide Pacific. Inside I was
American, and invisible; the shell
was Japanese, a broken cup. The drone
of an approaching plane filled my ears.
My fork twisted into the sunny-eyed pupil;
the yellow yolk oozed across buttery drippings.
"See the atom bomb," I said.
"Bombs away. Bombs away."

WORDS FROM OKAYAMA

Dear Sister,

I sit here hours. I do
not pray for sun or rain,
but for no full moon
and clouds to warm us. Father
has left; I've sent the ashes
by boat. No one's left
for me. My needles lie
like old anchors under
the current of memory.
Do you remember, Sister,
the apple tree we climbed.
King apples, how sweet
the taste, even now.
I've patched all
the clothes I can
and carry water to
neighbors for rice and tea.
I've no meat. I thought
the food in camp was bad
but it was better than spit
I swallow until my tongue
dry as July mud almost
swallows itself. I could
almost swallow my words.
The ones I spoke when I heard
that like unthinking cattle,
uncertain, afraid, docile,
we'd follow orders. We had
no more than we could gain.
Your son must say No.
Learn the good word.
There is no way that
he can be a man
without a sense of where
to cut the barbed wire
and cross the fence.

Dear Sister,

Thunder woke me in father's
house. I heard his hammer
slamming nails home before
our brothers were born.
They are the sum of us.
I've bought a hibachi for heat
and wool. I am the sum
of your money orders.
An earth tremor removed
the back wall. My abode now
reclines against itself.
I apologize I too must lean.
A fever has had me in bed two
months and now your money's spent.
I teach English when I'm strong
but farmers don't want to pay.
As if my American words had done
the bombing, they shy away,
or spit. I've chosen to live here,
but they don't see the reason
I stay. This is my home. Now.
I have no other.

Dear Sister,

Thank you for asking, but this
traveler could never return.
I've made my mark and can't
erase the smudge against
my palm where ink has left
its pain. I've left what
I thought was mine. You have
your life. I wish I had
a reason for every act; one hopes
someone will notice a traveler

whose eyes are crossed, whose
skin is creased with scars,
whose ankle twists against
her will. It's still raining.
No one notices, because
we're too busy
starving.

Dear Sister,

Thank the eloquent ever-being
for my eyes! Last week I beheld
a storm caught in the divide.
The storm leaked light
until darkness began to vibrate.
I feel that light inside
even as I write this.
It pulls at me until my feet
have no root to hold me
to this pasture. This year
I have socks and a quilt
to keep me warm.

BAILEY GATZERT: THE FIRST GRADE, 1945

Miss Riley stands above me, fading fast
beneath the porcelain light that frames her face.
Her finger, raised to God, declares each word,
each careful pencil mark must fill the void
between the faded lines. She measures us
the way she measures words like *brother, house,*
like *sister, sky* and *dog.* The way she measured
Stanley by standing him against the chalkboard.

The words are always only hers. She draws
the list and keeps the rules. The sky is bruised
but never green, a house can be magenta
and sister pink but never yellow. She matches
objects to their hues. We learn her world,
but she is never part of ours. She would
never walk down alleys, never visit
one room homes too poor to invite a guest,

or running water, a stove, or ice. She hawks
us in the class. No boy dares laugh or talk.
An easel slants its errant legs as if
to trip the unaware; we tiptoe past it.
(Three long snows, a gift from Franklin D.,
has taught us how, without apology,
to live behind barbed wire and journey home.)
We learned to quiet trembling mouths and hands.

Words contain our thought. They tell just who
we really are, or camouflage the fool,
the quiet stranger who lies behind the smile.
One day, I whisper, "Benjo....Benjo." I try
to tell her what I mean. "What did you say?"
Her question rocks the room and laughter sails
on wings about my ears. She checks her list.
No *benjo* there. "O-benjo!" I can't lose

control: frustration pools a cadmium stain
across the floor. Miss Riley turns, her silence
a naked finger: enemy! I've mixed
American and Japanese. She rakes
her memory—does she hear the dying cries
of boys who toppled easels, erased the sky,
then grew to manhood on the way to war?
My hand's raised to heaven. I'm here. I'm here.

Agoraphobia: After Camp

She pulls the front door shut
and turns the key until it's firm.
She pulls the blanket close and
stands behind the curtains,
turns the radio low, and watches
the gauzy world sway and
pass her window.

Children play across the street;
they hit a ball before the cars
arrive. When the ball hits
her window, it rattles like a
lost pigeon flying unseeing
into a mirror, like a neighbor
wondering when and if
anyone is ever home.

When someone rings the bell
she sits in silence until
the steps retreat. The shades
are pulled; even at dusk
she keeps the room unlit
so no one passing by
will know how slowly
a day can pass.

Call screening keeps the voices
from the outside world
from entering past her phone.
She has enough of visitors
who won't remove themselves.
Fingers in her ears will not
remove their cries.

Does she savor every
moment and every breath
of every second of every day?

Even in the dusk of living
the wrinkles accrue like taxes,
her hair a thinning testament
to that life islanded against the world.

PART II
PLAYING CATCH WITH THE PAST

Playing Catch With the Past

For Brooks, Yosh, the Team, and Rev. Andrews

The 1920 hand-me-down baseball glove my father gave me
was so thin I could feel the stitching on a ball thrown
with childhood fury. Burnished with Minidoka dust,
a kind of Trapper, it snapped sharply when it snared the ball.
The second glove I bought from my Baptist basketball coach.

"Go up the street and compare this glove to theirs," he said,
"and buy the one you like best." I bought from him because
he trusted me like a father to make wise choices, to pass
or take a shot, snare a rebound and make decisions in seconds.
I chose his, walnut rich and proud as a teenager's pomaded hair.

Our choices make wins or losses. Fifty years ago
the preacher's son decried his father's divorce, and joined
the unforgiving voices who tossed his father from the church.
The team sat in silence caught between sensibility and god
and tried to pull together like cords in a raveling rope.

In 1953 the father drove a blue Chevrolet bus of ragged city
children down the California coast, past the redwood
giants, through Petaluma, Santa Rosa, The Golden Gate,
names that draw images and smell of time now dead
in summer-filled memories: this is where the team began,

where boys learned each other's names, earned their God and
Country awards, their merit badges, and discovered
girls and religion were manufactured in different countries.
Now divorced and remarried, the son today preaches praise
for the father's deeds and love for those who gave the boot.

During WW II, The Blue Box or its father bus
traveled from Seattle to Minidoka fifty times, and maybe more.
The mission of a missionary is to carry the Word of God,
not sewing machines, saws, hammers, nails and ironing boards.
A missionary of action is a propagandist without words.

The Buddhist families remembered the mission long after they
    forgot the sermon.
His funeral could have filled three churches.
I still have the glove, oiled and oiled again, almost ebony
from age and pain. It's been found time after time
in one box or another. And the finder always says, "Look! Look
    at this!"

Gathering grit and balls of dust, the glove returns this year
from the pocket of a closet so deep my arms could not reach it,
almost a miracle on a day I'm about to go to the season's first
    game.
When I put the mitt on, I punch my fist into the pocket,
looking for something hard, a screaming grounder from the past.

BASEBALL SESTINA

We're sitting here at Safeco, high above the bases
waiting for the game to start. The paper fans strike
the thermal air but cannot drive away the heat.
Anticipation stirs between the aisles. Olerud's swing
disturbs the atmosphere, and Cameron fields balls
that stray within the park. We're hoping for victory

because we've lost enough to know that victory
in small doses must last a lifetime. The simple basis
for such a minor homily comes from ball
games played in fields, where workers could strike
against the war by picking onions, not balls, and the swing
of a shovel could shake the earth and create daily heat.

Across those farm fields rose dust in waves of heat
as Sekio and Itchy came to bat, fighting for victory.
Fathers, brothers, uncles—each took solid swings
and looked with longing when they saw empty bases.
Across the ocean, brothers without rifles struck
Paradise beaches with every syllabic spitball

that they could muster. They'd rather have a baseball,
play catch than duck grenades, while the Tule Lake heat
changed families into prisoners who faced more strikes
than they could swing at. No chance to play, no victory
could be won even with runners loading bases
if the batter has no opportunity to swing.

Some brothers and sons took the chance to join and swing
the tide of war, lost their lives but brought the ball
game home, where those behind barbed wire loaded bases,
knowing the right pitch, curve or change, or even heat
could bring fifty years and a measure of victory.
These actions in ten dusty fields today strike

pride in grandsons, granddaughters, too young to strike
against the pain of '44. Yanks swing

their bats against a Mariner victory;
Sasaki and Hasegawa pitch Japanese ball
against Godzilla, cheered by half the city. The heat
they feel is not of war and death, but loading bases.

When Ichiro raises his bat, prepares to strike the ball,
his swing, clean and measured, creates its own heat.
It's victory we want, but first we need to run the bases.

SADNESS IS NOT A RIVER

Sadness is not a river that flows through the daily plain;
It is a flood that has overflowed its banks and reaches
Around every rock and deep into the roots of ferns
And Douglas fir, into crevices left by army ants and bees,
Where it sits soaking into the horizon waiting for a flame
To ignite the quiet depression that is drowning its victim
In the oil and kerosene of private immolation. Where is Joy,
The beautiful long-legged demon of youth that draws
The eyes of men and women alike? Where is June,
The queenly creature that soars through clouds, her fiery eyes
Ablaze with the spirit of sunrise? Gone, for Time has
Overflowed its aging banks, overwhelmed by the rush
That accumulates from months of snows. When day reopens
Its morning window, my mother rises like the winter sun,
Struggling through the foggy thoughts and ailing vision
That blur light and darkness into ordinary gray.
Although summer light has faded, the pain
Of rising and falling must sustain each day.

PURPLE HEART AT 93

Since 78 she's fallen
once on the beach,
taken three stairs
and a header against a wall,
cracked three ribs,
been bruised from shoulder to hip
broken three fingers
seen them bent sideways
seen her kneecap shattered
and removed after a
tumble at Southcenter Mall.

She's fallen on the neighbor's step
(another finger) too busy
talking, not watching,
a tumble on the grass
(thank god, nothing broken),
a collapse backward on the gravel
looking at the blue hole
in the sky, wondering,
who tipped the world?

A little tipsy not from drink
but toes that weave themselves
into a basket, cupped
like a Chinese tea cup,
toes crossed for luck?
no wonder twenty-eight
steps down to breakfast
every morning feels
like twenty-eight predators
praying for her.

Asiatic Lilies

Their odor heavy and foreign fills
the mailroom like the scent old ladies
wear to cover the smell of age.
When I turn I find a vase full of
Asiatic Lilies, a floral fall of color
that reminds me of the hair and dresses
of crazed elementary school teachers
in their purple or orange hair
and pink and fuchsia dresses.

What craziness filled the halls as
women in unspeakable and unnamable
costumes laid down the law of
propriety and good behavior. Their hands
engendered an order and a silence
I can't get to the bottom of
as I watch my own lilies lean
toward the sun under the apple tree.
It's weeding time, time to dig

on hands and knees under the tree
where memories raise their puff-ball
heads head high. I can't just break
the stems, so I dig with my trowel
to loosen the roots, and finally with
my fingers, probing the moist earth,
inhaling the smells from composted
fir needles and bark, separate
the good root from the weed's.

This getting to the bottom takes
lots of effort. Hands and knees gritty
and marked, I pause to survey the work
and change they have wrought in me;
I shape the unnatural order now
their blooms are done. When they bloom

with purple highlights and apricot colors,
I'll praise them not for beauty and order,
but for the crazy clamor they raise each summer.

THE VISIT: KAWABE HOUSE

Pretend your mother
has put glue on your
chin and you have in-
advertently touched it
to your breastbone
now the parts are glued
forever and your eyes
search the ground
and find no horizon

pretend your gym
teacher tells you to
roll from the top of
your head and to
continue that roll
until you stop just
above your belly
and you become
asparagus or bracken

fern just emerging
in spring in this
the winter of your
new life you look
like a question
mark the place you
hope to reach but
before you take a
step let your body

twist so slightly that
your shoulders roll
before your hips can,
now, roll your
your body right
until you're left
with your left

shoulder where
your right was

and your head
replaces the crook
of your elbow
and locks you
halfway to where
you came from
and never where
you want to go
in this your new life
at ninety-five

In Memory of the Yokohama Express

For Jr.

Jehosephat lies stiff as a crust of bread
beside the garage, a palm-wide trail of ants
already pouring from his ears
and eyes across the curled leaves.
Lisa and I carry the corpse up the hill
where five nights before we buried
two stray babies. David follows,
dragging a shovel, come to dig the grave himself.
He tamps the dirt with his hands
then tramples it firm. This rabbit's death
is clean. But grandfather's been in the hospital
four weeks and dying tonight. His sweat
soaks the sheets, and they're pumping his lungs
as if he were a drowning hull.
Lisa sits stunned and whimpering.
I who had little reason to mourn as a child
hold in awe her grief and pain.
From a time before farm yards and houses
her miraculous agony carries into the air.
David comforts his older sister,
cradles her as if she were the baby, says,
"Lisa, it's okay. He's happier now."

SON'S JOB

This job isn't like hacking necks off chickens
and opening them up to purge out the guts,
dipping the feathered bodies in boiling water,
wiping off the feathers and hanging the bird
on the conveyer belt, a job you can't get far
enough from in space or time. My job asks
that you heat the tube on both ends until
the wax softens and the end wrench can loosen
the caps and the lenses come tumbling out.
Watch how each lens shaped uniquely
has its own face and order that you draw
like this for memory's sake—an easy way
to forget the hot feather bath. The alcohol
instead of steam, wiped across the lenses,
shines them, no streaks, no smudges,
and you reassemble it a lens at a time,
following the pattern you've drawn on paper.
You look down the barrel into the past,
the blurry vision of a father's work to raise
his child comes into sharp focus.
Hold for a moment, the scope to your eye
the end threaded with hot wax,
the vision caught.

Summer 1958

The echo of cannons, the Friday
night smells of hamburgers, hot dogs,
and French fries boiling in the fryer,
the rumble of balls down the waxed
hardwood floors before the explosion
of pins, coming together down Beacon
Hill, Jackson to Second Avenue,
neon shimmering through the slick
windshield, a Friday night foursome
to roll perfect games in the upstairs alley.
Nishikawa, Kanetomi, Kaneko,
Sanbo, Naganawa, Nishimura, Hirota,
roll up their sleeves, hike up
their ankle length skirts, bobby
socks white as an empty score sheet
in rented shoes smelling like old potatoes,
heft the balls for X's and slashes.
No dancing for open spares
and unhappy splits. Not a gutter ball?
Cheers for Martha! Cheers.
Smoke curls into the lights.
Mark the scores: a high of 125,
whata-game-u-got-tonite!
Mystery pin setters slip from alley
to alley, taking shelter behind blockades,
rolling the balls back to the scoring benches.
No one hears the rain outside;
no one feels the storm whipping
through the naked windows.
Lightning strikes. The neon blurs
and in the darkness above,
dangerous clouds cast
no visible shadows.
Throughout the rest of our lives
the cannon sound of thunder echoes.

Bookseller: David Ishii

1

Wise Pioneer Square owl roosts behind
the high top desk; when we walk in, the books
all seem open to us, free to look at and touch,
no guardian to keep them safe from salty fingers.

But ask a question and a flutter of feathers,
the hat and glasses—the eyes—peer
over the desk, and the words roll out
one after another, far from a simple WHO

but a dissertation with overtones,
a Ravi Shankar of conversation, corner
stone of the square, pinning us against
the books and held by the spotlight of words.

2

Drove by today, almost the last day
of the year, lights were on, shelves
showing bare, and someone with the hat
sitting behind a desk, Alan Lau's

sign still in the window. 50% off
and nothing left to sell. It's a sad day
when the place of memories is the place
where the lights go dim.

Thirty years ago, every AA writer
who'd published a line or read in public
lined the stairs and walls. This place
marks the beginning of awareness.

3

Saturday's rainy weather may flood
my island home. It's time to fill the sugar
bowls and salt shakers, time to shake out
some good luck over the table.

Vashon Island will find me at the garbage
dump throwing out the refuse of the year,
putting out the lights in the empty room
and making sure the doors are locked.

Never Sleep: A Portrait of Jackson Street

I am 85 years of darkness stalking
the streets on stilts, reaching for the moon.
I am a one-wing rooster with the heart of a cat
stalking himself on corners and busses.
I am a pigeon gurgling in the snow
and when I snore I am an old sow
waiting for piglets to suckle her.

I am all things in the middle of night:
a tadpole in summer mud struggling down feet,
a child singing "Sweet Chariot" in a choir,
Uncle Remus peeing in the gutter,
a rooster full of stories, bleeding in a barrel.
I am you, waiting to drown
in sleep's cradle.

Children fear dreams I leave in their heads.
They feel the tickle of fur and feathers,
fear the heat and pinch of fang and beak.
I hibernate in metaphor
and wonder what will waken.

Moon shimmies up the legs of night.
Lord, Lord, I cannot strut.
Body's weaker than its skeleton.
Cat's quicker.
I'm sweeter than a lemon,
lovelier than a raisin.
Like the moon, nightly
I unsettle this street.

I am Never Sleep, whose
voice is full of creatures.
I have seen myself
in the mirrors of your eyes.
You name me the color of night.
No wings to fly, sometime

before the electric dawn,
may fog drift through morning
and carry me into
the long and lonely day.

WHAT CAN WE LOSE IN SAN FRANCISCO?

For Frank Chin

Legend says a troll thin as a Chinese lion's tail lies
asleep elbow deep in sawdust beneath the stage
Frank Chin sweeps south of the Golden Gate.
When with fingernails as long as fingers, I expect him
to ask for leg of lamb or raw goat steak—
the stuff real trolls feed on. "Goats?" he says,
"I love goats only after midnight, and then live and sassy.
It's my belly I need to fill."
We search our hands and come up with nothing short
of eating our words. Maybe there's something in them
he can chew or swallow. He hauls us by the script
into the office, drops page after page
into the coffee pot, adds onions and dry vermouth
to boil for twenty minutes. "It's the way I like it,"
he says as he picks them out, still steaming,
one by one, and pries them open.
The broth drools down his moustache; his teeth sparkle
like broken shells as he bites down. There's a little
sand there, but what he chews, his harsh molars
grind into praise. We depend on him to tear
the voices from our words and take
what we have caged so carefully on the page
and belch them on the stage.

LEE SIU LONG: LITTLE DRAGON LEE

"Though dancing needs a master, I had none...." Theodore Roethke

BRUCE LEE—cha-cha-cha
BRUCE LEE—SI-FU
CHA CHA, cha-cha-cha
KUNG FU Dancing Master
PUNCH to the Stomach
BACK FIST to the Temple
SIDEKICK—to the GREEEEEEN HORNET?

BUZZZzzzzing across Seattle, 1962.
You carry your girl with a nail in her foot
from the garbage dump 347 steps
like she was a sack of Long Grain Precious Pearl Rice
(loving her in and out of her sack...CHA CHA).
Smooth as wonton slipping out of soup
down Chinatown—the DRAGON ENTERS
across the ceiling of Little Three Grand, dazzles
waiters with three pecks to the eyes and one
on the forehead (for good measure) and ORDERS
HO YAO nGAO YOK FAN, meaning Crazy-Cow-on-Rice
if you're tone deaf or Cow-Covered-with-Oyster-Sauce on FAN
if you can sing it on key.
Even Charlie FLEETFOOT halfback Mitchell was slower
than a muddy field across the cross-eyed fingertips
of Brucie Little Long: LAO TSE forgive our decay
and WING CHUN our chins seeing us cha-cha
and double-triple kick across the YU DUB campus
YIN-YANG KUNG-FU TAO.

Little boys and old men today say
"Next to Le Siu Long, Ali *may* be the greatest."
But in my head you are who you have always been—
foolish star grasper leaping across ceilings in a single bound,
wolf trying to shake the house down,
tongue-twisted twister speaking English English with a
    Chinatown palate,

lowdown happy slapper, something I still see a flicker of
when I watch your movies for the fifth time.
There you are, faster than celluloid,
more powerful than a zoom lens, and I am flying
across 20 feet of bathroom in a 15-year-old movie
the same day you met head-on with Theodore the BEAR
ROETHKE, who said, "I'm Roethke the POET
and you are in MY ROOOOOOM!"
to which you said, "I'm Brucie Kung-fu-you-in-the-eyes-
and-in-your-bad-knees Lee and I am using this room
to teach my girl my kung fu kind of poetry.
Shake my hand."

And the next day big Ted said he had met you
face to face and BEARS was no match for DRAGONS.
CHI-SAO—cha-cha-cha.

I even thought I could cha-cha, but now I write this
what I call poetry to funky music—would you believe
TOWER OF POWER? It comes from somewhere, old friend,
Dancing Master, this dancing and fancy footing around the
    stage, which begs the question:
WHERE HAVE YOU ALL GONE?

The Little Three Grand never sounded like the Chinatown
Restaurant it No Longer Is.
Ted Roethke, who needed no master to fill the skies
with a galaxy of poems, has drowned in a swimming pool
after playing to a crowd who watched him fall
all day into the pool crying, SAVE ME. SAVE ME.
And the star you reached for has fallen
in your lap, coursed like fire through your veins
and exploded like a cherry bomb in your brains.

but LISTEN!
Chinatown! Chinatown's dancing, Brucie,
to the crack of your forearms on the teak

scarecrow manikin skin because you said
CHINESE IS NOT PIGTAILS
and they have followed your winding tail from
San Francisco to LA to Hong Kong,
seen you become a meteor, little dragon,
dragging everyone out of their restaurants,
their back alley cardrooms, their MAHJONG-brick
hotel rooms because you had
LOTUS PETAL TOUCH/PRAYING MANTIS SERENITY/
    MORE LIVES THAN A CAT
and spent them all proving you was a MAN
when no one doubted you was just like them
in spite of DRAGONCLAWS/SCALES/FIREBREATH.

So they are stepping not to the cha-cha
or the bugaloo, not the waltz
or foxtrot or polka—
they are jamming in the streets
from the Japan towns and Chinatowns,
the refugee towns and migrant towns,
a winding trail of immigrants
who are the American Dream. They are the muscle
and arteries, the scales and claws,
the dream and nightmare of another DRAGON,
its tail careening blindly
BANGing and CLANGing
down your street and mine.

Sukiyaki Mama

For Amy Sanbo

*A choreopoem for the Johanna Weikel Dance Company; choreographed
by Carl Yamamoto*

You press your face against mine
as if I were a window into the past.
Your reflection melts like wax
down a candle. One eye disappears.
Your nose smears into your chin.
Other days you are stone because
multiple sclerosis corrodes your nerves.
It short circuits your hands,
cuts them off from the world.
You say you're in a box you can hit
with your elbows, but there's only empty space
where there should be walls.
"Pull yourself together, it's only MS."
How do you pull yourself together
when you've lost the strings,
can't be sure you're standing on a ceiling
or a floor, can't feel your face
or your children's hands?

    Once you was a little sukiyaki mama
    troddling through Chinatown. . . .
    Chinatown, where old men could hardly
    keep their old skin on.
    Brucie Sifu Lee warned lightning
    and the bus boys that you was his
    little short grain pearl of rice.
    You ran the street, and at the gambling house
    the watchman at the peephole unlocked
    the door and pointed out the game.

    The lady at the corner table marked
    the play with her cigarette until you won enough.

The gamblers threw your numbers, gave you odds,
when you called odd, enough to pay tuition.

You won a wad from a five-foot pock-faced gambler
you later learned earned his living
killing men. He only smiled,
thank god.

They're gone now. Brucie's ashes.
Chinatown's almost clean.
You're bare as a wire, inside
and out, and you have multiple sclerosis.

Hey, smile a little. You were free
then, like rain across a pane of glass.

You funkied down in black town,
went grooving down the hall with Tiny Tony Smith,
sang "I Was There When the Spirit Came"
at the First A.M.E., otherwise known
as the African Methodist Episcopalian Church.

You *bon odori'd* round in Japan town,
served *sashimi* and hash on skid road.
You waved pom-poms at money town,
signed contracts over dinner at the Regis,
said, "No, thank you," to a ten thousand dollar evening
because your body's worth more than bucks.
In Harlem a Greek restaurateur thanked you
for jiving the fire out of seven riot angry hoods
who never heard you sing but felt your spirit.
It was like grooving down the hall again.

You have claws quiet as butcher knives,
a mind single as a stalking tigress'.
Nobody touched you until you touched them.

I say: Let there be Light!
And flip the switch.
There you are, telling me Jack Matsutake-what's-his-name
is some fan-tas-tic dresser.
Underneath you could hardly stomach the lies
you spooned on the platter to persuade yourself
there's gotta be a reason to love a boy like that.
And when there is no reason good enough
you say, "Good night, Jack," and stroll away.

I say: Let there be Rice!
And there I am in your duplex kitchen
looking straight on into a plate of rice fried brown
as a mud pie, wondering: Can ketchup cure this?

I say: Let there be Bach!
And your stubby fingers raise from the keyboard
a fine spray that soaks my clothes, stuffs my sinuses
and lingers four weeks in the plaster.

Now, your hands are lead weights.
You have to ask if the pan is hot
or if I'm shaking your hand.
We chuckle when you drop your cigarette.
"I'm clumsy," you say, but we know
something's eating at you like an ugly
rat that won't quit until it dies.

Soulpatcher, you know enough of stone
to last a glacier's age.
You reach into the stranger in me
to find your friend, turn what is cold
and unfeeling into love.
You mirror the fool that I can be,
eat my heart as if it were magic.

Nothing's impossible in a world
of Believe and Do.

This is your hand, these your fingers:
flex and squeeze. These are your feet,
this a floor: step across and hope
for pain. But you do more than step.
You challenge the world of Can't and Won't.

You don't die because you're holy
and don't believe a world
your body says is vanishing.
Yours is a world of imaginary seas,
impossibilities, and dragons. In the desert
between us, it seems a lie,
but when I hold you, the sea whispers
and a dragon flaps wings into salt air.

MR. COLOR

For Bill Mair

He's Mr. Color; he's our color commentator,
Colorman, collar man, collard man,
he's the green mean man who mixes energy
with a viridian grin wide as Lake Washington,
who scares little kids out of their imaginations
and grows imagination in kids the way some people
pot pot in their potpourri barrel gardens;
he's every shade of the color wheel,
blinding white inside and hairy, hoary white outside,
all color rolled into one, spinning on a point
thin as laser light; he's fine wit sharpened
with an orange edge, one-upmanship and magenta
magic in a field of cadmium wheat,
olive barley, and yellowing corn; he's every
bit of bit and glitz, atomic particles
of intellectual matter gathered in enchilada
imagination, a stormy maize tortilla,
fiery, crimson peppers seething in gathering
clouds that furrow his brow,
that lighten a Payne's gray mood to
cerulean sky; gowned in Scottish plaid,
a crisscrossed landing field from which
humor wings like vermilion mosquitoes into
a smoky sky; his laughter squeezes air
like bagpipes across the office courtyard;
he's the world's clown but nobody's fool,
and everyone's friend.

HOUSE OF DREAMS

Somewhere in the ghetto sat a house of dreams.
Somewhere in the ghetto there sat a house that dreamed.
You could find it in a meadow in the middle of the ghetto.

You could find it in the shadow of the sagging wooden flats.
You could see it leaning on its heels, a little tipsy, dying
in the deepening light of a damp and foggy afternoon.

Like an aging senior citizen, its pate a little bald,
its skin's all scaly and wrinkled splotchy in the weather.
See, its door has opened to the intruding August rainfall.

When you come across the house of dreams, swaybacked and
        troubled,
waiting for the angry reaper of the night, you'd want
to roof it, shingle it, and raise it straight, but the rubble

would rumble through its belly and tremble in the mist.
Past its open door lay steamer trunks and toys, like jewels
from a treasure chest, at the end of a long, long quest.

All this, in a little house, in the middle of the ghetto,
where the fabric of everyone's life was wrapped in newsprint
and stored with dreams of faery queens and dancing marigolds.

Here were books (somewhat softened by the fog), a photograph
(a little shredded by a mouse), bags of twisted nails,
and a stack of cloths chewed into the shapes of hearts.

Here were towels that caught the "Oh" that fell from mouths
when Uncle Rosie granted a three-year rest; here a hand-
        stitched quilt
stolen by mice who raveled it into personal, private nests.

When you came upon the little house, you found the trunks'
sad bottoms already burning red with rust and grinding
slowly into dust and mud and coffee grounds.

Who would save this sad, little house of dreams?
Who could take the twisted nails and straighten them?
Who would stop the rust, and shine the dreams' bright dimes?

Somewhere in the ghetto sat the house of dreams.
Somewhere in the ghetto there sat a house that dreamed.
You could find it in a meadow in the middle of the ghetto.

This was a little house that housed a mother's dreams,
a house that's now a shadow of the dreams that flowered
in her mind. Greying stacks of kindling are its remains,

for someone's sledged the sagging walls and trucked the trunks
and broken timbers to the dump. There's only silence now,
and no one's raised a voice, nor have the birds begun to sing

for all the dreams that flowered fifty years ago,
for this is the house of dreams that's no longer a house,
but a vacant meadow that sits in silence in the ghetto.

I Deserve So Much More

Dear Teacher,

So many expectations I had before I entered
your class. I already knew how to think and
research, but you want me to paraphrase
without telling me the code hidden in
every statement I'm supposed to crack.
How can I footnote without putting the note
at the foot of the page? My toes curl when
I think of the days I spent to understand
the secret code of MLA. The Missing
Language Association buries its secrets
in books that only my research could find.
I spend 40 hours a week trying to figure
what you want, and shouldn't the grade I receive
reflect the effort I give? Of course, I never
name the people; it's not my style. I use
third person and always speak the truth that only
I know. Your opinions and theirs mean nothing.
I don't need them in my gated community
of knowledge. I am who I want to be. How can
you fail me for the run-on sentences
you say I'm supposed to know, when you haven't
taught me how to write a comma splice? If you
won't teach me what I need to know, I'll have
to teach myself. I know best what I need
to learn. It's as clear as the apple in Eve's throat.

Thank you for reading this,

Your Anonymous Student

LOVE EQUALS INSANE LOGIC OR OXYMORA RULES

They've been doing nothing, they claim, but their words
are as arresting as diet ice cream and there are even odds
no amicable divorce will work, for any smart fool can see
there's no safe bet that love can survive the minor miracle
or the freezer burn of pandemonium and the burning cold
of quiet chaos that survives between star-crossed lovers.
Like caring Republicans the couple cleans the dirt
about each other with accurate rumors meant to stab
the other with the dull needles of false truths.
Their lives are written in invisible ink and dressed
in loose tights. No peace force of friends can create
the hot chili of passion needed to even the odds
that their disinterested love can survive. Give me a firm
estimate, she says, of the free rent it will cost to be
part of your life. And he, in turn, admits with the insane
logic of rehearsed improvisation that she is good garbage.
Let us, she says, turn a blind eye to all we have done.
Yes, he says, turning a deaf ear to everything she says.
Tomorrow they will create a mud bath of words
with which to cleanse the insane logic of their lives
and should they fail, they will bathe in the joy
of forced freedom that a clean divorce will provide.

THE PIG AND I

When I need a body part, I will look
for you, who are my compatible mate.
We share heart parts and even the flu.
We can walk together along life's high
road or find a home in a slough.
Life is an adventure in eating; built for
omnivorous dallying with incisors,
canines, and molars to grind
red meat, roots, and stews—all
part of the daily meal. Give us salmon
or tripe, even the other white
and our stomachs will be satisfied.
Like lovers we share heart and lungs,
spleen and stomach filled with
blood and the same air, bile
and the daily moment. Whatever
you can share, bone or blood,
I'll take; when my parts need
to be renewed, I'll meet you at
the feeding trough, wear your
DNA and appetite, and grunt
my way through life as I
have always done.

SCISSORS, PAPER, ROCK

Jan Ken Po—scissors, rock, paper—
music murmurs from every stone
like spring in winter's yellow light;
one fist settles atop the other,
like vertebra on vertebra,
an act of faith and chance.
When something rises, something falls.

Jan Ken Po—paper, scissors, rock—
The chisel frees the shape of stone.
Art remakes the world by degrees.
A pencil remarks the angle of the arm.
A hand draws flesh across the coldest stone.
The dancer's pirouette attracts the light;
calm ascends from fury.

Jan Ken Po—rock, paper, scissors—
When art wraps the moment's anger,
song is loosed to search the sky.
Words take the shape of fire
and float like signals from the hills.
Color values the eye; the spirit
finds words, color, sound and stone.

MUSEUM

In the city museum I touch a three-foot
container coiled in Japan, theoretically
used for water. I climb in and wait.
The museum doors close and lock me in.
I stretch my feet over the lip and hang
my head out and doze. A movement
to the left catches my eye.
Other feet and other ears appear at the tops
of jugs. Even the smallest ones. I choke back
a cry as they emerge from urns and cracked brown pots,
some in kimono, some in happi coats, and some
naked, breasts leaning like bunch grass before a summer storm,
one foot uplifted and held before them
like hands. Fans gauze their faces.
I call, but they walk right on by.
Eyes in the paintings smile. Their lips invite.
The bodies gleam moons glazed with the ashes of darkness.
When I give chase they slide behind a curtain
and turn in to the folds of dream.

SONG FOR LOVERS

Whenever he rolls her onto the bed
the people upstairs move. He knows
because the chandelier rattles.
He wonders if they hear them love
and decide to join, being too old,
too old to do.

Whenever he opens the front door
down the hall another clicks closed.
Sometimes he races to the door
expecting to see a fragile
figure bent eye high to the knob.
He never does.

In the laundry room someone
is always adding clothes to the wash
or taking sheets from the dryer.
He lies awake dreaming that it's
the husband's private detective.
How would he know?

The hall has ears. The ceiling eyes.
The light outside the door burns off
and on whenever they arrive.
The lovers burn; their sheets are moist.
And above them, the building whispers,
"We know. We know."

HUSBAND'S RESPONSE

Lips stitched to heal the wound
your words have caused
keep me from spilling what's
festering. You'll need a scissor
or knife to open them, to let
the venom pour, and I need
your lips to cure what sours
in me. That's what partners
do: Cleanse the ill,
for better or for worse.

Beach Talk

Or on the True Nature of the World

Sandpipers and sanderlings squabble
over little details crows and jays
rail over. Rain chatters to the tide
pools. A sand dab beaches itself

from the receding tide. I counsel
it back into the Sound with the edge
of my shoe, and shaking itself as if
to confirm its multiple personality,

it merges like sand into watery desert.
While rain converses with air, creeks
from high bluffs sort through the crash
of old trees. Loquacious as drunks

in a bar, they carry discourse to the stones'
angled corners and clay's marbled face.
Each few yards another creek blathers
to all the brothers and sisters clouding

the atmosphere, about to plunge into salt.
More water! More water! Sand sucks my feet
like a geoduck. There above me, three
wing-flaps and a long glide away,

drifts an eagle, her white cap
a snowfield against a granite cliff.
I slog the beach. Her white
head scans the horizon and me.

I would follow her to the aerie,
but she disappears. In her place
a fledgling circles, brown wings
edged with night, and is circled

by a gang of gulls and jays.
Their clamor startles even
the tired weather. Outnumbered,
the fledgling circles and ascends.

DEPARTURE

The ebbing beats of the diesels should slow
to a gentle humming. Instead
my heart pulses salt water.
Its leaky valve jerks irregularly
through the cycle of blood
and shakes this house of seas.
Rain slashes; foam roils like froth
along bared fangs. Confusion
squeezes me tight. The stars are lost
behind my eyes. The starboard leans
to port. The windbreak windows rattle
like words incessantly matching act
to schedule, coin to deed. My mind
rattles like a snare. Where flows East?
Where West? The large barge roars
under its breath then treads water
while behind us the black city shines
like a new monster. I've been waiting
for days, watching the weather change.
As diesel under pressure builds
and explodes, I struggle from
the wooden piling where water breaks
beneath the prow—or is it stern?
and wade heart-high into the deep
that hides the moated castle
under restless, slumbering waves.

The Face of Water

The splash of water on your face
recalls the rush of water over
rock, slowly shaping each ridge
and curve. The roar of rain across
the porch clatters like loose rocks
collapsing from old cliffs too weak
to hold themselves together. Old
tales tell that water in the hands
of torturers reshapes the faces
of men too brave to cry. As I
hold a bucket of rain too green
and old to drink, the moon clears
the clouds, and I delight how its pale,
unworn face shimmers in my hands.

HIGH BANK

Freedom catapulted over the hill.
We hesitated, skaters thin on ice.
She muzzled back as if to say, "How'll
I lead if you're afraid?" The mud and moss

step the slick way down to Vashon beach.
No guard rail. No rope to hold us to the path.
Returned, a long-haired shaggy creature, she eased
our wavering fears across her back, strolled past

slick stones and crumbling bank to the long edge
of beach and water where she finds her name.
And, later, you said, "Freedom, find an easy
path for us. That hill's too steep a climb."

Freedom nosed into the brush as if
to map another path. "There's no path there,"
I corrected. "Let's return the way we
came." I braved uncertainty into the air.

"Trust her," you said. "She'll show us where and how."
"No path. No, none. This way I know," I turned,
with Freedom straggling back. We heaved uphill,
tortured courage, carried resolution

to the top, where sat Ole Anderson:
"There's an easier path back to this place.
She comes up right there by the picket fence."
Your eyes bruise mine: "That was Freedom's way."

October on Green Lake

The geese know me, I'm sure,
by my overcoat, perennially bad knees,
and my brown bag of crumbs.
They wait each day until I sit
on the park bench. Then they come
squalling out of the lake like pigs
to the trough, their bills
clothespins shaped after fingers.
One large bird goosesteps,
a small eddy at the back of the tide.
Its left leg lags. The flock opens
where I'm about to step and fills
where I've been, but the lame gander,
too awkward to dive straight
misses whatever I throw him.
My sack's empty too soon. When the geese
gaggle back to the lake, the lame bird
disappears in the cross current of bodies.
They barge into the mist and the maze
of cattails. In the silence they leave,
I catch the drift of winter.

WOODLAND PARK ZOO

We bring our children to view the animals
in their civil wilderness and watch them
romp like orphan gorillas through their hoops
and pipes. Families of proboscis monkeys
preen in the midst of apple cores and oranges
tossed like grenades across no-man's land.
"Why are they fighting?" asks Todd, pointing
to the tortoise who lurches heavily across his mate,

their heads lifted to the artificial day,
their incandescent sighs winding through
a plastic eternity of evergreens
as the other single Sunday parents parade
their charges out the door, intent on
discovering discreet polar bears
who beg marshmallows under a sky
bereft of sunlight.

My son sees with four years' knowledge
his parents have reduced their lives
to a civilized truce. How can anger sizzle
like a couple in love? My arm ropes him close,
but the world twists out of control.
Divorce is a word with jagged edges.
I have no fence to save him from lies
that thrive in a counterfeit wilderness.

SUQUAMISH BEACH

1

Barefoot, we pick our paths across the beds
of sharp shells and stones. We kneel
awaiting the tide and the flush of small
fountains. The children, too, dig
for clams, except my son, who sits
crying on a rock, islanded by the crush
of shells.

We haul them by their necks.
Some we cup cleanly in our shovels.
Others we raise, their shells
shattered by the accidental blade,
blindly believing they have
locked their jaws.

2

Little one, it is easy to handle clams.
They wear their skeletons for skin.
They have so little life.
I have seen my father suck them dry
on the spot.

3

The pale stone of the moon rises,
a scallop in its evening tide.

4

The clams are dying,
their shells half open, toothless
gasp. Their tongues
loll, thick and pale.

We sharpen knives
hunched over the buckets.
Clam after clam we scrape
each shell, and the soft
mucous of their bodies slips
into the crisp enamel pot.

The shells we drop casually
into neighboring trash.

5

All day the children have dug.
They play in the mud of our shelling.
Their hands are soiled.
The yard echoes with their sparse laughter.

6

My son stands in the center,
no longer crying.
He has tentatively joined the crowd.
His hands close on an empty, hinged
shell, his puppet. It gapes
his laughter into long waters.

During Divorce: For Todd on His 5th Birthday

You sat and colored in your book
all day coloring reality from dream.
Now you stay in the lines, use peach
for faces, red for tongues,
brown for the fur of wolves and bears:
things we teach.

When you face a blank sheet
you draw lines clearly human.
Your sun still smiles
but your wolves are all fang
and your elephants are lonely
for the bodies you draw off the page.

As you grow older, instead
of new lines as inflexible as
"ought to" and "must" someone else will
teach you to paint out by painting space in,
to flatter with color

the raw reality of black and white.
But for now, you settle back.
It's so hard enough to fill
the space you draw
around yourself.

READING WATER

Light raises its hand
whenever I strain to enter
the deep. What's real
tugs at the roots of questions.
Unpredictable snags lurk
like snares cloaked in glittering
leaves. Water rippling
and unreadable contains
its personal secrets.

Whatever rises rises
wingless like a nymph
in shuck undergoing
the watery blossoming to dusty
miller, olive dun, or ephemera.
Water refracts the other world.
As their wings unfurl, rough
water speaks diamonds crushed
in the glint of teeth.

The lure of darkness draws
me to its electric skin.
How many lifetimes before
a sleeper awakens? The circle
of water continues to circle.
What's hidden swallows
when they swarm from the hatch,
rushing from water,
to startle the air.

MILLION DOLLAR MYOPIA

"Throw away your glasses, kid. You got eyes the rich pay a million bucks for—one eye to read with, the other to drive."—words from a friendly ophthalmologist.

Lovers who press against my cheek
blur in my left; but my right adores
each pore and slips into craters
to lather in perspiration.
The myopic one enjoys the slow moment,
the texture of sheets, the dot matrix
that hovers over the letter *i.*

Oh, a lover of itself in photos, it screws
inward to avoid obvious truths that deny
the lie of life grown dull with old
lovers. (A good eye reviews the shape
of a body's circumstance.)

Dazzling in the other orbit is
my hypermetropic eye, a long distance
gazer who roams the miles, alert
for danger in side-roads, pot holes,
and broken glass. It rests on old oak
limbs or sails beyond on lightweight wings,
intent on bringing soft, furry creatures close.

Resolved to be in control, the long distance
gazer divides the calculated symmetry
of my smile, reveals instead wall-eyed
confusion when its close-eyed partner purrs
"Stigmatism!" (Stigmatism uncircles the globe.)

It's worth a million to be at once short-
sighted and visionary without creating
a serious spectacle, to read the world's
epitaph against a smoke-filled dome or adore
the languid tour of snail or beetle
through patches of thyme and basil.

On nights when loneliness descends
like wrinkles in my shaving mirror,
like switching ends of a scope,
the distasteful world disappears
in the pure, blinding twitch of an eye.

PART III

THE ROAD HOME

Minor Miracles

I see a mother stumble, a child in her arms;
she protects the child but strikes her ribs.

A blind beggar smiles, hand outstretched.
When I pass without giving, he says, "God Bless."

A ninety-year-old woman sits in ninety-degree heat;
others come with hats, umbrellas, and water.

Rain falls in the middle of the hottest day.

Angry people surround a quiet man, who listens
to every voice, his eyes welling with tears.

My friend is losing weight, 50 pounds and more;
I see change happening where it can't be seen.

One candle provides a meager but sufficient light.

Artificial respiration brings the dog, strangled
and breathless, lips already blue, back to life.

Someone sits in darkness, breathing.
Morning filters through the edges of the blind.

The old woman, doubled over with osteoporosis,
asks, "How are you today?"

I can hear chimes sounding a wind-blown melody.
A dog stolen and lost 6 days finds his way home.

I stand at an uncertain cross street.
Minor miracles make me tremble.

IN MEMORY OF VASHON ISLAND STRAWBERRY
FARMERS WHO MADE THE ISLAND SO FAMOUS
WE HONOR THEM WITH A FESTIVAL THAT
CONTINUES EVEN THOUGH THE STRAWBERRY
FARMERS WERE FORCED TO RETIRE BECAUSE THERE
WAS NO ONE LEFT TO PICK THE BERRIES.

Seen along the side of the road, a sign:

U-PICK
SPAGHETTI

RIP Charlie, 2003

Dead five days, said Wilbur of his dog,
while mine has disappeared into the wood
and I've spent three nights unsettled by
his disappearance. Already past fourteen,
his hind legs dragging across the porch, this doggy,
dog-eared tramp of a dog has captured my heart
and my fiercest fears. Vanished under
the house, burrowed deep into the forest?
No medicine can cure him from the sleep
he seeks. Having traveled all paths that lead
away, I've all but given up, when I decide
to travel to the beach, a fifty foot fall
from the house, where I find him, a quiet
spot on the sand, staring at the waves
as they roll in, lapping one over the other.

THINGS THAT SEE THROUGH YOU

1

Santa Claus runs his fingers through your hair and asks,
"Are you a good boy?" He will search what lurks
in your heart. No matter what you answer he says,
"Speak only the truth your shadow knows."

2

Your doctor asks if you've been exercising
and you tell him that you work out every day
by walking to class and you practice meditation
by standing in front of your students, breathing evenly
when they stare blankly and have no answers.
When he hears these words, he merely stares at you.

3

I put my foot into the fluoroscope to see the bones
in my toes, metatarsals fanning like a fish spine.
See, my mono-color foot wriggling in the shoe!

4

The man who sees through walls, iron vaults,
bedroom doors saves victims from the pestilence
of foul play. When Lois looks at him, she sees
steel, but when he looks at her, does he see
the beauty of her face and breasts or evil cells
that will chase her down the alleys of her life?

5

The big circle circles your body, winks and inches
toward the feet, all the while looking for the weakness
that is you in the density of your bones.
The CT scanner beeps like the robot it is, saying,
"All is well today; tomorrow will bring another set of troubles."

6

A sensitive wife always knows when a female student
sits in your office day after day, asking questions
like what do I need to take to major in American
literature? She knows when you take the long way home
over the Green River bridge or through Algona.

7

When you are five your mother
knows when you fail to clean your room,
put your dolls on the shelf, unhook the train cars
and unplug the transformer or change your underwear.
Your mother hears of your demise before you do.

8

The future is a blank wall you can't see through.
It's a wool blanket or an opening door.
What you can't see when you open your eyes you see
in the dark waiting for morning light.

THE FIRE IN MY BLOOD

Tule Lake 1943-1946

1

The fire in my blood has turned
my heart to ash. I am char and dust
heaped on the frozen floor.

No one has given me a stitch of power to sew
the scissored remains of my life together.
I am a heap of rags.

They've raveled what I've sewn
and stolen my business of cutting cloth
into the shape of other people's lives.

When they draped my clothes over their bodies
and entered doors I could never enter,
they displayed my hands and eyes.

I entered doors I will never enter and never see.
I've seen lives I can never live,
and now, callous disregard dampens the ash
of undrawn patterns; nothing left to salvage
the person I had measured myself to become.

2

You who have husbands and wives know
your angry spouse will relent and open the door
when anger slides like a stone to a tired stop
at your toes. But a lost lover won't
come home when darkness falls.
A lost lover will find another, softer hand
to hold his, will turn his back
on the memory of arms willing
to forgive him time after time.

3

A designer conceals the body's shape
with the drape of cloth and reveals
with loving stitches what the model
would never herself reveal.

4

What can you say to a lover who
refuses to look you in the eye,
to acknowledge your place
at his side, who does not introduce
you to his family, who will not
remember your name nor speak it
when he embraces you?
What should you say to a lover who
will not say he loves you yet demands
your love be physical and substantial,
who demands you give him money
and land, food and understanding?
What should you say to a lover
who will not cross the river
to visit you when the spring thaw
opens the land to young sparrows,
deer in the marsh, and white
blossoms of the perennial pear
but sends you away to a land
barren of hope and water and says
this is not prison but the gift from fear
that no one else can provide?

5

When there is no answer the best answer
is silence. When silence is forbidden

any answer is the wrong answer, but no answer
can satisfy every neighbor and the soldiers

who stand at the gate, who direct their rifles
at those who have no voice.

There are two questions and two answers.
Yes, Yes. No, No,
and no answer can be no answer.

6

The voices I hear in my head
toss my mind into a salad
of sour despair. When I awake,
I find real people behind the clamor.

I see that needle and thread
will not repair the rip that opens
when my neighbor threatens me
with his hammer, pitchfork, and
his maniacal eyes. His fever
is a fever no god can cure. Its contagion
works at me throughout the nights
I spend in this dorm for single women.
No answer will send me from
this prison to a prison in Okayama.
What can I place on the altar of
consolation to appease the renunciants?
Life has consequence,
and Father is dying in another country
where he searches for peace and sisters

he has missed for 40 years
of farming in Algona.

7

The wise woman knows when
she should build her own house
and how to lock the doors
of her heart. But for 25 years
I've left the gates to my
heart unlocked and open.
Unmarried, but a union made
at birth confines my role in this
journey Father has set me on.

8

Death will knock at Father's door
before it knocks on mine. I'm the last
left to care for the old man, to mop
his perspiration, change his clothes,
feed him soupy rice and cuts of turnip,
and swab his open sores as he lies on straw–
no mattress, no wooden floor, but hard
cold dirt ten years into the future.
If I could see what would happen
I would still choose to leave the stranger
who restrains me for the father who has
abandoned me in this naked land
where disagreement is king and reason
threads its way out the guarded gate.

9

When your lover asks for your hand
you make a choice to fall into his arms
and remake your life in his

or turn on your heel and continue
to walk the direction you were going.
But when your lover shows you
the door, the choices narrow
to one or nothing. Well, he did
not demand but opened the door
to say, "You may return the ring
I gave you when you were born,
if and when you decide to leave."

10

Some days I open my door and find
my neighbor's voice casting stones of anger,
a cacophony of bitter words I do not deserve.
Other days, the doorways are empty,
but a voice resounds in my head.
I wonder if god is knocking on my head,
but when I look for the handle, I find ears,
and no door behind which god
can stand or hide, or even recline.
God, I could use a good man to put my life right.
But men, like my brothers, have always raised
the timbers of their houses,
built roofs to stop the light
and bolted the doors against
the night and its rodent intruders.

I want my door open. I want to remove
the roof and stare all night at the sky,
and the revolving lights that circle
the exact spot I stand.
When the snow fell last night, it was
like light falling from the sky.
Insubstantial light became substantial;
transitory light caught the edges of my fingers
where I held a thousand lights

like miniature candles. I hold them now,
my offering and, yes, my life,
here in the wilderness, one woman
singing like a coyote among
eighteen thousand lost and angry crows,
shouting at no god.

11

Silence speaks nothing in my ear this morning,
as deafening as snow that fell on my fingers
the night before. I search for crows
but the darkness that covers my eyes does not
shimmer like the oil slick of feathers.

Is this peace the death of day and the beginning
of night eternal? Has god visited my bed
and cured me of the assault of voices that nailed
accusations into my brain? I am no whore
for war, no *inu* for America, no bitch for peace.

What Japan would sweep me into its arms
like a lost fiancée returned after an angry dispute?
I'm the bad relative, the tossed and rejected virgin
looking for a broom and crumbs at the back door,
hoping my feet will fit slippers too small

for even this fallen angel. The peace I feel
at this moment balloons through my imagination.
I'll take needles to my ears and eyes
and wait for the explosion that will bring light
to eyes already blinded by faith in my country.

12

When lightning shatters the ice of silence
that has held me for seven days

and thunder rattles my eyes awake,
I am pulled from the darkness that swallowed me
into the diamond brilliance of a morning death.
Will it be me or someone else?

A halo of crows greets me and flies
across the land. I pray for darkness
to drape the valley. Spring's light
blinds a future where death
lies around any corner.

13

Doctor, the bud of pain appeared when I awoke
and began to spread as I crawled from
the government cot. As the day spread
its glow across the winter sky, the little bud
opened into a dark flower growing deep
and wide into my spine and down my legs.

As a child I inherited a bouquet of black
blossoms the day I fell from the rafters in the barn.
I lost a summer that year in pain, enduring
Mother's remedy, lines of fired incense set in dishes
lined along my back, that colored the air brown,
and sucked cockroaches of despair from my mind.

Doctor, by nightfall, the pain had vanished
but my legs were wooden stilts on which
I could no longer walk. I stood, but balance
walked out the door and left me against the wall.
I slid to the floor, able only to pull myself
into a chair, where I sat for two days.

The knotholes were friends that talked in rough,
cold words to my fingers until a neighbor noticed
my mess hall absence. That's how I came here,

an unfeeling vase of blooms stuck in this infertile land.
You must believe the paralysis is real, that
the wrens and crows pecked at the windows
when they saw I was unable to fend them off.
They would have entered in summer when the doors
were open and taken me to their nests
a peck at a time. Last night something entered
the hospital ward, its wings created a stir,
and the air cried out: Away! Away!

14

When the world is too much to bear
I close my eyes and disappear. Watch, and see.
When the chatter in my head grows
incessant, I search first to find god's voice
because he's always hiding in the lettuce patch.
I raise the volume on his voice until
it drowns the noise. I can't tell what
he is saying because he sounds like thunder
that broke across the sky last Wednesday.
But I have my knitting needles by my side
in case he falls asleep, takes ill, or dies.

When the world was too much to bear,
I asked Father to carry me
from room to room in the farm house
he built by hand the year that I was born.
I shut the doors as he carried me
deep into the house, where no light shone,
where sound became a flickering light,
and the voices lowered to a low murmur
like quail grousing in the fall fields.
Of course, I know there's no farm house
here, only the sawdust on these thorny
slivered floors where I lay myself to sleep.

This morning I counted the bits of dust
that grow in the corners, before they could
seed and take the wind like the cottonwood tree
behind the farm house. I broke the windows
one summer day, when the sun burned
through my shut-tight eyes. Father boarded
the windows then, and light grew dim
and the shadows around me disappeared.
See, here is a ball of dust, and there a dark
spider slides into the split between the boards.
The grains of sawdust are really red ants.
I will follow them under the floor, into the earth.

15

Some say that dust can clog the lungs.
The dust that hangs over this room
is black and gritty, as coarse as sand.
Some mornings I feel it mask my face,
an angry, beady grain that desires
to enter my body and multiply.

This grave morning the black dust buzzes
in my ears and circles overhead like a hive
of black bees. I blanket my face and curl
from the window. I look for darkness
to wall the bees but light screams across
the room. I am drowning in the noise.

I release the body into the sounds
that surround me. Breathing in and out
is an easy motion I never think about,
until the dust congests my lungs. What I
inhale through the charcoal atmosphere
purifies neither the air nor me.

I want to live forever but daily life
is a conflagration that burns like the coal
in the iron stove on the south wall
of this room I am dying in. As fire transforms
coal to dust, so may it convert
these hands and this heart to stone.

THE DAY AFTER

Two weeks ago, I awoke to frozen weather.
My muscles were fragile as popsicles.
My bones rang like empty pipes of copper.

I was frozen out at home,
The power was gone; the heat died.
We sat in a tundra of silence.

I'd been waiting for warm weather,
so I decided to help the thaw, agree to concede
my role in creating stubborn frost,

clean the house, start conversations,
break the budget for the perfect gift,
a furry coat to warm the weather.
Then the rain hit. The wind stormed
like bad temper, garbage cans dumped
in the driveway, glass shattered.

I stand here, cleaning the mess
alone in the rain. My shoes are soaked
and my socks are damp. I feel my toes

disappear in the bone-deep damp
that reaches under my clothes.
Water rises to my ankles

and I sink in the muck. I'm growing
shorter. My doctor asks,
"Something eating at your bones?"

CHECK UP

A stroll into the doctor's office should be a slam dunk.
An easy pass from you to the doc and a no-look
behind-the-back affirmation that you're adept
enough to hang around the key, or float
your way to the three-point line for an easy swisher.
When the ball leaves your fingertips, you sight
along the rim and see the ball drop out
of sight before you lift on your toes, release the ball,
and follow the arc that reaches like a long finger
from the half circle of your follow through. Something's
trying to score against you; and you play defense
holding illness at bay, knowing your strengths
and playing to them, driving to the hoop, passing cleanly,
leading your center as he cuts through the lane.

Shooters say you must see the shot in your mind,
see the ball fly through the air, an angel
swooping for the nest. That same imagination
sees your life run a hundred years. "I'm a member
of the hundred-year club" my father said before
he died at 75. His imagination,
at least as good as mine, kept him healthy
9 years longer than I have already lived.
I take his pass and see clean air, clear water,
sunlight shimmering against glass and over the shallows.
There's something brown in the air over the city
through which the dark towers of skyscrapers
struggle. I see it like a bad brown foul made
without regard for the penalty shots I'll get.
Like soot that covers the white roof of my old car,
it scrapes skin raw, sandpaper removing one
molecule every last second of your life.

Elegy

What can we remember of an old man who died "before his time"
Because he drank too many beers, ate too many chocolates
  and pined
After too many women but never caught enough to keep alive?
He might have had another twenty years but he preferred life
Unfettered by doctors and their prescriptions for staying alive.
Who remembers the memorable words he spoke each day?
  "I'm fine.
And you?" "Nice day." "I love the rain." He thought fog would
Help him find himself. He went to work each day, came home
  in the dark,
But he never said anything to change the world, to wipe
The rain from anyone's life. He walked down a street named Main
And smiled and tipped his hat, if he wore one, to every passing
  woman
Thin or thick, short or tall, young or old. The miracle is that
  each smiled
Back at him but never remembered if she had ever seen him.
And he would look ahead searching for another pair of eyes
To catch his eye, to say I notice you, you are real and alive.
Barely a man, he almost sighed before he died.

BALLOONS

When air withdraws, balloons return to rubber.
Fully stretched, with bloated bellies, they float
And bobble on the air like dust on water.
Deflated and empty, balloons lie lifeless, flat.

When lungs balloon with air, they blossom, bloom
With every breath, for life depends on inhale
Exhale, inhale. When stale air fills the room,
Life pales, for every inhale should be full.

My aged mother snoozes all day long.
Her breath moves in and out without attention.
Then one lung deflates. She's left without song
And air when panic pinpricks her body's balloon.

Thus casual life takes on a deadly stare
And she must find the calm that's choked by fear.

For Those Who Have Died

I think of those who find the rotting dead,
Carrion beetles, blowflies, vultures, and men,
Who feed on what is left when life's good light
Has dimmed and died. At night I see raccoons
Along the road's soft edge awaiting death by
Approaching cars. The stars de-light the sky.

One summer day, I came across a carcass
Spoiling in the sand, above the tide,
Pristine in death, 400 pounds now washed
Ashore. When three days passed, and at its side
I stood again, the flies now filled the air.
A week, and the stench was more than I could bear.

After a heavy rain, I found a deer
Quietly sleeping, neck broken in a fall
Of fifty feet from the cliff above, the sheer
Face enough to make me wonder, a wall
Too steep to climb, but such an easy trail
To a quick demise. Life, so swift and frail.

Some stray raccoon lay moldering in the grass.
My dog had dragged her home two weeks before.
Guilty or obsessed with smell? No more than trash,
The carcass became the smell that some dogs wear,
Like Obsession, Chanel, canine Clinique. I never
Said a word; I took my spade and buried her.

When death rose through my house, I searched the walls,
The basement, along the pipes, and there I found
Caught between two plastic pipes, swelled
Like a fat balloon, a rat its teeth clamped
Around an electric wire. Shocked, I backed
Away. Maggots would empty the body's sack.

Almost late for my father's funeral,
I drove two days to meet the obligation
That death had consummated five days before.
His face raised upward from the casket open
For inspection from passing, careless eyes.
He lay a day; we sent him to the furnace.

FALLING MAN

For Jason

What's it like to climb a ladder and take a step
across the empty space between the rung and roof?
What act of faith the ladder will not slide
and the roof will have the will to hold your weight
as you ease from one embrace to another?

When you reach out and no one takes your hand,
can you assume that faith will bring a lovely stranger
to cradle you if you should slip and take a plunge
headlong into the abyss that awaits you and me
in the dream of an uneasy and uncertain height?
Even in the broadest day the snare is there,
an apparent safe and solid step, but blind confusion
for the unwary, who trusts someone's hammer hammered
nails true, that the roof is not glass, no mirage, but solid
as tar. Who among us will take the first step?

Our eyes deceive, subtle liars bent on playing
the mind like a fish on a fly. Too much line—
we recognize the slack; too little and we
sense the trap and snap the line. God, there must
be a god. Must falling be hook, line, and sinker?

In the middle of a fall, do you catch yourself,
send a signal to your brain crying "Emergency!
Emergency!" or do the wrens stop chirping and people
stop talking? Does time signal time out? "Time Out!"
you cry, your arms reaching out to embrace yourself.

Or do you give yourself to gravity, open
your arms as if to embrace the air? To be
a kite that hangs and flutters in the wind
as it winds its way toward the clouds? Or opening,
a parachute drinking air like a fat stomach?

Gravity always wins. Imagine stretching out
to greet it as it draws you in, curl and roll
as if gathering energy and releasing it
in a long rushing scream of white water.
Wherever there's pain there's still life.

So you hope for pain and dread it. Each embrace
has limits; what reaches out may not save you.
Man needs air before water, they say,
so the next breath is all we pray for.

PEACE

When the blanket covered the house
it swallowed the light and chewed
sound into bits that scattered
through the forest. Branches cracking
made a sieve of silence.

When I walked out the door, the day was
grayed by foggy inspiration. No birds sang
in the firs, the sun struggled through
the wavering branches, but light, though
frail and doddering, prevailed.

When silence entertains with its shadow
of sound, and the darkness of the day
provides illumination for the
perceivable moment, life settles into
its recliner with nothing but patience.

HONEYMOONERS BEFORE EXTINCTION

The Honeymoon

What little smile, little twist of the lip,
what frown, what whisper, what touch
of the fingertips alerts him to her
anticipation of what's to come? Does
she move across the seat and put her
hand on his thigh? Does he glance ahead
along the yellow line when love catches
itself in a crack of desperation, the smallest
door that opens into the night that
never ends, the crash of thunder that
sits like a cat below the water tank
waiting to pounce, rapt with silence?

The Road Home

The long road home runs faster than the flight
of bees. When you cross the imaginary
line from high plains wheat land to this
land of bracken fern and fir, something cool
like summer's last breeze slides down your back.
In the deepening dusk that half-dim world
swirls with insects rising from summer's dust,
then fused by impact to the glass. The glare
of the setting sun is reduced to a haze, and
the weary hours weigh heavy on the eyelids.
The joy of home fingertips away, you struggle
to keep alert to the roaring passage of semi-trucks
and laughing teenagers as you race down
the switchbacks on the mountain interstate.
Life, you know, is perfect; your love dozes quietly
beside you. And you can see life laid out like a map
on the hood of your car. This is the moment
Sleep, like a gentle sniper, closes your eyes.

Home

The winding road back to Jojo's home
is like sailing against the wind, a never
ending thrust against the current that
wants to float me back to the mother
I've left in an empty house. As we speed
down the highway, toward his mother,
whom I shall meet for the first time,
I stare at this new husband of two weeks—
and wonder who I married. That first night
was tungsten to my magnesium. I imagined
I was a Swedish fire starter who needed
no kindling but this cool husband
has me stymied. He's immutable and tough
as wolfram, not quite gold, but gentle
and caring like the finest cream on
my skin; he's never flustered, confused,
nor does his temperature rise even when
I test if somewhere there is a man
who will stand if I fail, who will hold
the sail and change the shape of the wind.

My Name Is Joseph

Why does she call me Jojo? It's my mother's name
for me. I'm Joseph, not Joe or Joey. Changing names
makes me a chameleon trying to blend into whatever
wall I find. I'm not who she thinks I am. She wants
to know my mother. She wants to sit with her at tea,
to taste the crumpets of our lives. Instead she'll
see that long hallway opening to rooms filled
with old trunks and dark furniture draped in blankets,
rooms dim with failing light in a building as gray
as the lives they have lived. I've moved into
the brilliance of early noon where my eyes are blinded
by possibilities. That's who she is—my wife—my

possibility and future. She is the hook that pulls
me out of this swirling confusion of history, of failure
without a future. When she opens her eyes and sees
the hotel, when she opens that door, will she see
the broken plates, the tarnished forks, decaying chopsticks?
She will smell the mold of lives trapped
in the tunnels that we call home. She will see
the mouse my father is, and how my mother
has led him through the maze that is our history.
And she will see what I really am, like my father,
blinded by the light of possibilities and confused
by the forking paths this new life presents.
I'm trapped by my possibilities and my indecision.
I would be content to lock myself
in that warm and comforting darkness.

Her Words Are Little Knives

Why are her words like little knives that
thrust themselves into little painful avenues?
This marriage I wanted stretches before
me like this highway we have been traveling.
It's full of pot holes and potential rock slides.
We're too close but not close enough.
Skin to skin is too much like a locker room
congregation to be comfortable. Her eyes raise
welts if I don't bleed. Is marriage an allergy
between two unlike beings? Her cream curdles
with my green tea. I am an American even if
her mother doesn't think so. I can't be the man
she wants me to be. I do not use words as
missiles. I am my mother's gentleman, and
I aim to be hers as well. I move aside for her,
open doors. If we had lasted fifty years we'd
be there now with you, looking at our faces
in the mirror, wondering how we made this
journey scarred but alive and holding hands.

TREASUROUS SLEEP

Sleep's treasure is a pocketful of change.
Its music turns to silence in the dawn.
Sleep journeys through waters calm and uncertain.

The melody lingers in the drowse of awakening.
Those fingers that fingered my hair leave it askew.
Sleep is a treasure, a pocket full of change.

Stepping to sleep's shore, I slip a toe in.
The chilly water eddies, no smile, no frown.
Sleep journeys through waters calm, deep, and uncertain.

No question that wading into the surf needs strength,
for water can hold you under until you drown.
Sleep's a treasure like a pocket empty of change.

When thunder rolled throughout the night, it warned
lightning was prowling, before it struck my house.
We hope for calm water, safe journey, uncertain

that we will ever float, or breathe again.
It takes faith to close our eyes, and fall
into that pocket of darkness and endless change.
The last sleep journeys through waters deep and certain

ARS POETICA, MY ARS

1

After the heart are artery and vein.
Filling the channels with venom will be in vain.
The more you say the less you mean.
Close the mind and let the word mean.
Be athletic.

2

Using scissors or an eraser won't make you athletic.
(Math brain fires synapses 40 times a second.
Athletic brain fires synapses 40,000 times a second.)*
Start thinking
to be full of Un-thinking.

3

Puns are the rotting fruit of language.
Rotting fruit makes juiced language.
Ambroguity is the favored beverage of the muse.
"No ideas but in things," says WCW's muse.
"No ideas" means No-things.

4

When can nothing be everything?
When it's less.
Unless, of course, it's Un-less.

---

*unsubstantiated "fact" that made an impression

PRE-SPEECH

My mother's face presses against mine afraid
that what I haven't said means I have nothing
to say, that the words she shares are garbled
in my brain, that I am mute because I hear
silence. She leans so close I can feel the heat
from her breath and words. She is afraid the future
will be an empty wall, that I will spend my days
believing that the wall is as full of life
as a book, or a zoo, or a school. Look at me,
she says, with love in her voice, but her
eyes fall away like channels I could fall into
and never return from. My father's voice rises
and falls in measured strokes, but anger measures
the metronomic rhythms, for he expects me
to be like him, to open my mouth, to engage
with others like cars rushing down the freeway
he drives me on. I know you think it's strange
a child without language can put these words for you
to read, but you can read my words in my face
and eyes. When you watch my eyes, they will touch
your face and slowly wander toward the window
where the words shine from my eyes and vanish in the glass.

HE LOVED HIS FATHER

He loved his father but he wanted to love
fishing more, so he waited while his mother
dug through the worm can to find the wriggler
that would mesmerize a hungry trout. The child
was patient while his mother stretched the worm,
then pierced it twice as it curled its flaming body
around the metal ornament. The child fished
from the bank until his feet hurt; the spray
drifting from the river gathered in his hair.
Every nudge meant a possible strike, but
his hook was bare. Try eggs said his father,
who loved roe as much as trout. When eggs
failed, his father peeled larvae from the rocks.
His father knew how fish moved and tasted.
He was used to little deaths the river passed.
The child stood on the safe bank of the Cedar,
his thirty-inch rod reaching over the rushing water
while his father walked through water, his cast,
a shining missile in the morning mist. He watched
his father reel in flashing rainbows and unhook them
flopping into his bamboo creel. The child watched
his father walk the stream, thinking like a trout,
luring it from its deepest hiding spots, following
the stream, chasing the river until the child could
feel himself searching for the rainbow's silent refuge,
he could feel the hypnotic pull of the bait wriggling
through the water, and even though he had felt the sharp
barb of the hook, he could not resist its magic
as he felt himself drawn by the current toward
the dark and blurry shape that had been his father.

No, Misery Loves No Company

No, misery loves no company even on the saddest days
When air funnels down to a stream so thin, a needle could not
    pass;
When muscles refrain from moving because just sitting still
Creates a marrow of ill will in the bones; when facial skin feels
Two inches thick and so calloused, a hand on the cheek
Is a dull scrape on someone else's skin; when air rasps
And water gurgles in the airways.

No, misery loves no company when your dog crawls
Across the porch in so much pain he is ready
For the silent needle; when your parent has died of a long
And complicated sadness; when work turns into one
Dullness as gray as a hundred days of rain;
When your love decides that living in another city
Is the only way to find the sunshine missing in her life.

Misery needs no company, for it is a narrow path
Full of mysterious turns and potholes, a journey
One struggles along in search for the way home.

Body of Evidence

Here is the body of evidence laid out before us.
There across the floor are the shoes that left the prints.
And here and there are the hands, stretched open;
These are the culprits that did the deed, broke the window
And pulled open the closet, manipulated the safe
Where her heart had rested in the safety of imagination,
Reposing in the dark space that she called home.
Here under the jacket, in the chest, lay the intent
Of the perpetrator beating like a little drum, a battery,
That moved the hands and feet. And here, under my hand,
In this hard skull, lie the plans he schemed into an intricate web.
Wrapped around him are the hand woven shawls
Created by the lawyers, meant to conceal the figure
Or shift the observer's eye from one shoulder
To another. These are the lines of the case.

We the jury sit impaneled in quiet isolation.
We have observed the heart pulled apart, its pieces placed
In evidence of callous intent. We have heard the argument—
How beauty raised passion like a stake in a heart, how love
Entered the equation, an X-squared instigator of choice and
    action.
Did she say yes for passion or love? Did he offer love
To negotiate the contract, and renege on the obligation?
Did she offer her body and not her heart? And did he own
What she had offered? For in that night that he had attempted
Possession, she had clutched him to her breast
And wrapped him in her arms without a red ribbon.
Now we the jury are faced with the mirrors of deliberation,
To determine our place in this plot, how we share intent,
Action, and punishment, to hang or be hung.

CLOTHES MAKE THE MAN

When we old men disrobe, we reveal what we truly are:
Indescribable humanoids, troglodytes and homunculi,
Neanderthals and missing links with hair like tufts of grass
Struggling to stay alive in beach sand populating the plains
Of aging backs. The ocean of skin is filled with rising islands,
The color of decaying humus. Beach balls, flesh colored,
Stretched by heated air, contain the body's lardy hubs,
Their blow holes tied and protruding like pregnant women's
Belly buttons, wide as fifty cent pieces. Every bottom sags
Like two deflating balloons wrinkling in the cooling breeze.
As if hanging from strings, they barely bob, but clench
So they squeeze and droop like the cheeks of aging peaches
Molding on a window sill. Human bling hangs,
A variety of lengths, some placed so delicately
They are almost invisible, receding into fern filled,
Dank caves. No joy-filled sight, these bodies on spindly legs,
Knobby arthritic knees, needing aluminum walkers and canes,
Struggle into chinos and socks, shirts and jackets and ties.
But when they stand, wrinkles disappear; their poplins creased
And clean. They comb what's left, put on their glasses
And face their feminine partners, who embrace their lovers,
Clean, handsome, and civilized with horizon-wide smiles.
They affirm the old lie about men and their clothes.

Rushing through the Gravel at 99

Picture this odd scene, little lady, no larger than a 5th grader,
Wearing sunglasses as wide as her face, hair tied up,
Until she is aerodynamics exemplified, crouched in her chair,

A little four wheeled sports car palpitating though the gravel,
Pausing to cross the handicapped lanes and dodging
Four-door passenger cars as they push toward Genesee.

I am the motor and she the controller of brakes,
Pitching and stumbling, often at cross purposes,
Wind blowing through our clothes, almost out of control,

And fat little me, hanging on as the little chariot careens
From side to side when pickups and SUVs brush us back
To the sidewalk. In the day's moldering heat we stumble

Across traffic heading for the blue of the lake.
Like Icarus lured by the shape and fire of the sky,
"Let's do it," she says. "There's not much time left."

PART IV

YOU MAKE MY SILENCE SING!

Father, because you've
carried me like a sack
of bleached bones so many years,
today I can string my pieces,
find flesh and muscle, a mouth,
words, my own needs. I've found
a head and sewed it on.
Tomorrow I strike across
this unsettling sand.

The steel trout
in the dying
river, unable
to throttle
the urge that
drives him from
the filigree
of his tail
to the last
jaw shattering
flash, enters
air on the hook
of his dream,
to be born
of water, borne
on air.

Lost in swirling
    shallows,
I rest where you rest,
attached until I die.
Let the tides flow on.

This is no life
sucking salt water
all our lives,
scuttling from one
stone to another,
afraid of light
and moving shadows.
Let's hook ourselves
to a brighter line
and flash our
bellies to the sun.

Ah, my gold-finned darling,
when you float from the depths
of sleep, the shine in your eyes
blinds my heart.

Bathe me in your love
and I'll rinse the world
from your hands.

I wear my skeleton outside
but you burrow through me,
a terrifying star that beckons
through water's broken light
to the softest parts of me.

I am any empty
horizon whose shape
longs to be charged
by the lightning
of your words.

Fish, flesh, and fowl,
you are my wriggling,
uncatchable, unfathomable,
most flamboyant, flighty,
delectable and earthy delight.

What's nosing around the dark
its moist nose probing
the knotted tangle
of wintered roses
scratching at their roots
and inhaling the mixed odors
of mold and old earth?

When they began to prowl
the lawn and excavate holes
large as eucalyptus trees
I saw that male and female
living in the same fenced
yard had made the electric
connection you and I have.
They succumbed, unsexed
and virginal, to the inner
compulsion to drive their
limbs into unyielding, rigid
earth, until earth and not
their padded paws gave way,
until the open pit became
an open quarry and they
tunneled through the dark
where, like us, they nest
in their invisible hollow,
a place so quiet and private,
only moles may visit.

My little mole, you've crawled
out of the dark, blinking blind eyes
to the light, in the continual struggle
to distinguish the leafy tops of trees
from their roots' spiny entanglement.

Stone love:
   Flesh against
   flesh, we strike
   again and again
   until we ignite.

Water love:
   Fill me
   until I drown.

Wind love:
   Invisible,
   you shape
   what I am.

Air love is
transparent,
plastic, thin
like a whisper,
won't crack
under rock or
hammer,

is light as song,
fills with sunlight
light; unwinds
ribbons of red
anger, glistens
blue, cradles
clouds,

surrounds
every moment,
doesn't weigh;
absorbed by blood,
fully fills
you and me
in every cell.

Like an old wind, love comes
and goes, a door slams,
a turn of a latch—

then you return—
and my heart
is struck anew!

I am earth.
You are spruce
who stands above me
in the salt air.
Your roots reach deep—
to touch my core.

Rain beating like fists,
wind opens its mouth.
I awake shivering.
The storm spills my mind,
and I cry your name.

I'm knotted and tough
as an old madrone,
but my love for you
grows slow and faithful
from scaly summer skin
to the deepest burled
ache of my bones.

I hold out my arms
and you blow through.
Fall leaves me unclothed.
I'm filled with icy weather.
I open my fingers and
you tie them into knots
then glove them in snow.
I'm rooted in this garden
you've planted me in.
If you'll cut me
to the crown, I'll grow
long arms full of roses
sweet as spring loam,
and you can nest
in the knots
of my fingers.

I've spun my snare
and waited,
a patient
spider
ready
to provide
the next
meal,
a cozy
space,
a comforter
of silk
for just
the smallest
taste of
you.

You are the last
robin in the nest.
Wings to fly
must find the air.

Even on wintry mornings
birds of the air
gather their wings,
and sing love. Sing love.
And so do I. And so do I.

We watch the rain
roll down the glass.
Our hands cup
to catch bits
of holy weather
for each day we've
lived together.
We have touched earth's
circumference and are
inextricably bound.
In me you see
the world's joy.
In you I see
its treasure.

I fill my lungs with bits of you
as you breathe in and out all night.
Each night we share invisible parts
of what we need and what we've used.
I am what you were, and you
become what I have left behind,
so you and I are not two parts
but a quiet connection in the blood
that feeds each cell, what binds
us through the years until instead
of two we breathe as one, dusk
in dawn, palm in hand, voice in song.
To name one is to name the other.

Oh, pile me high with hams and ribs,
roast of lamb and paper bibs,
julienned veggies, baked potato,
tomato, wild rice, and sour dough.
Butter me, knife me; oh, fork and spoon me,
slice your apples and peachy tarts;
lick me clean—oh, gorge on me
and my unflinching porcelain heart.

I am an empty plate,
scratched pewter, a patina
that shadows your reflection,
waiting on a bare table
to be wiped with the soft
towel of affection or filled
with your steamy, cinnamon love.

After we make love,
the embers quietly close
their bright eyes and you
roll away. Back to back,
the body's heat recedes
into the ineffable darkness
we hold inside ourselves.
We doze, like two pieces
of charcoal, dreaming separate
dreams until, in the sun's
dawn magic, your leg sprawls
across mine and stirs charcoal's
happy curse: though fired once,
we're ready to burn again.

You speak a halo of ideas
mixed into a chord of hues.
You sing a melody of colors
that races up my spine.
You sculpture feeling,
marble-smooth and cool
then forge it hot and malleable.
You spread love on the keys
and mix it on my palette.
Yes, overwhelm the canvas,
and nail me to your wall.

This love is full of scratch and scowl.
Love's voice tries to patch each fall
and keep us on our feet, and takes
your hand and puts it here in mine.
We survive not because you're you
nor me, but because of love that's
definitely sweet, granular, and Equal.

I am never sure which part of me
is standing across the room
when I am waiting for what I know
is about to happen.

If that's not me who raises
a glass and winks, it must
be you. But if this is me
with the brilliant smile,

then who is sitting there
knowing everything that's about
to happen? When I cross
the room, you do too.

I am sitting here, waiting
for you. Or is it me?
Don't leave yet. Yesterday is
Tomorrow in disguise.

I am darkness
without lightning.
No moon spies its
reflection in my cup.

I am wintry weather.
An icicle without
the sun will wither
like a plucked rose.

I am a kite
twisted in March.
The thread that holds
has begun to fray.

I am the emptiness
everyone avoids.
What I feel
must be contagious.

My love for you rages
like water over the falls.

Without you
I am a dark room
without a switch.

How many hours have
we sat and talked
the old words,
the old thoughts,
the old laughs,
each sprung fresh
by the moment
we've just stepped
across to plant
the first kiss
sunrise after
sunrise.

LET'S MAKE THIS MUSIC SING

Its black and white keys sit a half
Step between you and me. You reach
Across and whoever I am becomes the other
Part of you. You are the right and I am left.
I create the unresolved tension of a diminished
Seventh but you create a melody that sings
Me through the progression. Life can still
Strike a major chord, but your melody
Sings this counterpoint of mine through
Acrobatics of scale, with a little modern
Syncopation that keeps the beat from
Measuring time as if it could be counted
In pulses and seconds instead of amplitude
And color. We'll let this pitch and tone
Measure the quality of days and listen
For the joy that soars and falls, without regard
To the uneven metronome called heart.

SNOW BREAKS MY EYE

Snow breaks my eye into a thousand parts.
I juggle fragments in a world of snow,
and raise your face, a charm against the blizzard.

Against the glass and brain, your silhouette
has left its mark. I cannot shake your shadow.
Snow breaks my eye into a thousand parts.

I vibrate like ice struck by the shock of light;
a sudden chill collects the migrant floes.
I raise your face, a charm against the blizzard.

Light departs a prism and spreads my heart
like wings against the wall; light leads where no
snow breaks my eye into a thousand parts.

The slivers we are would make a painter's art
seem safe and simple. A jagged mirror will show
me raising your face. No charm against the blizzard

will change the fact that we will be apart
and yet reflect each other. Where I go,
snow breaks my eye into a thousand parts,
but I raise your face, my charm against the blizzard.

TANGLED TANGO

See the two who walk the floor,
step and close without the weight
of gravity, then close the door.
They Tango close, and pause, and wait.

The man must lead the lady's mind,
for he must be the liquid glue,
(like golden ore that must be mined)
and shape their bodies' lively flow.

And she must give herself to him
that they may move and pause as one,
a special closeness twining them
like golden threads of common twine.

When she decides to take his hand
she shares her energy and power;
if one should turn, both turn, extend
their circles, and forge a common core.

Is Love a Moment Lost in Vertigo?

Is love a moment lost in vertigo?
The dizzy spells appear and disappear.
Let's dare the old physician to say it's so.

The day I leaned to kiss you on the nose,
the world tipped and spun me on my ear.
Is love's best moment lost in vertigo?

As long as I could stand and dream, I'd know
my feet were firm, but then you smiled and shared
the words the old physician gave to you: so

long as passion fuels the body, throws
the heart off stride, and chews the cords of nerves,
love may be overcome by vertigo.

Almost forty years we've bloomed like roses
caught in a hurricane. Age repairs.
Let's dare the old physician to tell us so.

This world's a crazy top, a dizzy show;
our love will grow a hundred years, and more.
Love's no moment lost in vertigo.
I bid the old physician to say it's so.

NOTHING AS COMFORTABLE

Faces familiar as old shoes line the room.
Yours sits on a shelf
like a ten-year-old's first
ballet slipper, a smile almost.
Your mother moves the conversation
in two languages, one mine, the other hers.

I don't remember names, but they play
hana, "do *shigin*" and *ikebana*, and chat
once a week as five others did
in the $60 three-flight walkup you used
as a lover's nest nights your mother
was out of town singing.

If there are new wrinkles
I can't tell. I change languages
whenever the going gets tough.
I pass pictures of you looking younger
than your dancing-shoe face, and your son
naked in the swimming pool mistaken for a daughter
offends my pride.

These are the facts of the visit.
What is said is how good you look.
What I feel is how touchable you are
in your yellow California bikini tan.
What your mother feels
reaches into me, the words unstated,
her recognition. My best friend
I tell her. Maybe only friend. Peacemaker,
I would put you on, and you would fit only
as well-worn leather can.

About the Author

PHOTO BY DAVID YAMAMOTO

LONNY KANEKO was born in Seattle and spent his preschool years in the Minidoka concentration camp in Southern Idaho. He grew up in Seattle, attended Garfield High School and the University of Washington, and moved to Vashon Island in 1982. He began teaching in January 1963 and began full-time at Highline College in 1966, where he served as Chair of the Arts and Humanities Division and currently teaches writing classes. During his time at Highline College, he served on King County and Washington State Arts Commissions. He was also a member of The National Assembly of States Arts Agencies. He has taught English at Grossmont College and SDSU in San Diego, and recently at Shanghai Jiao Tong University. He has practiced aikido and currently practices tai chi on the island.

Lonny Kaneko has received both national and local awards for his poetry, fiction, and plays—including a fellowship from the National Endowment for the Arts for poetry. His book of poems, *Coming Home from Camp*, portrays life among Japanese Americans during and after World War II. *You Make My Silence Sing* was a collaboration with painter Camille Patha and privately printed. *Lady Is Dying*, a play written with Amy Sanbo, won the playwriting award from the PNW Writer's conference and the Asian American Playwriting contest and was produced in San Francisco (Asian American Theater Workshop) and Seattle (Northwest Asian American Theater/Asian Exclusion Act). Stories, poems and essays appear in anthologies such as *An Ear to the Ground, Daily Fare, The Big AIIIEEEEE, Asian American Literature*, and *The Seattle Review*.